Praise for *Belief I̶ ̶ ̶ ̶K̶i̶n̶d̶ ̶o̶f̶ ̶T̶r̶u̶t̶h̶, Maybe*

"*Belief Is Its Own Kind [...]* vom-
an's search for her m[...] story
of what we all long f[...] mily
and knowing how safe we are [...], [...] and
loved. Lori Jakiela's memoir is filled with heart-wrenching
scenes and moments of transcendence. It doesn't look away
from the ugly, but it always finds the light that rises above
it. To read this book is to experience our lives and their
complicated arrangement of disappointment, sadness,
wonder, and joy. I won't soon forget it; neither should you."
—Lee Martin, author of *Such a Life* and *From Our House*

"I am a big fan of Jakiela's writing, and *Belief Is Its
Own Kind of Truth, Maybe* has all of her gifts on full display. This memoir is sharp, insightful, sad, and often
darkly funny. Her prose is honed to perfection, sure,
but it really is her big heart and her wisdom about
the stupid, terribly imperfect, and beautiful world
that makes me want to read anything she writes."
—Greg Bottoms, author of *Angelhead* and *Pitiful Criminals*

"Adoptees look out at the world from the eyes of what
was lost. We can't help it, but we can transform it. Lori
Jakiela's new memoir—*Belief Is Its Own Kind of Truth, Maybe*—is a beautifully written journey into one woman's
process of letting go of what was lost, and the messy
dignity of human transformation. Her story is one of
life, of reaching for life. With a deep gift for storytell-

ing and unsparing, beautifully gritty self-examination, she brings the reader on the harrowing journey with her. It's an important ride, and an important book."

—singer-songwriter Mary Gauthier

"Brilliant, heartbreaking and fiercely honest. In *Belief Is Its Own Kind of Truth, Maybe,* adoptee Lori Jakiela tells a story of losing her birth family twice, yet creating abiding connection and love with the family she creates. A powerful, essential read."

—Linda Carroll, author of *Her Mother's Daughter* and *Love Cycles*

"'What is the nature of your search?' asks the Catholic Charities counselor at the beginning of Lori Jakiela's memoir. There is no simple answer. It is a search full of pain, vividly remembered or imagined details, and laughter—not all of it from trying not to cry. Jakiela leads the reader through her search for her birth family, the rejections, the struggles to understand, and the victories, and intertwines this with her memories of the sometimes uncomprehending parents who raised her, her discoveries about their wounds, and her day-to-day struggles as a parent to much-loved small children. No part of her life is easy—nor are the lives of any of her families. But Jakiela's spirit and voice and sense of the absurd keep the reader involved. I couldn't put the book down."

—Marianne Novy, author of

Reading Adoption: Family and Difference

Belief Is Its Own Kind of Truth, Maybe

LORI JAKIELA

AUTUMN
HOUSE PRESS

BELIEF IS ITS OWN KIND OF TRUTH, MAYBE
An Autumn House Book

PRINTING HISTORY
Atticus Books edition / 2015

ISBN: 978-1-938769-42-9

All Autumn House books are printed on acid-free paper and meet the
international standards of permanent books intended for purchase by libraries.

"Autumn House Press" and "Autumn House" are registered trademarks owned
by Autumn House Press, a nonprofit corporation whose mission is the publica-
tion and promotion of poetry and other fine literature.

Autumn House Press receives state arts funding support through a grant from the Pennsylvania Council on the Arts, a state agency funded by the Commonwealth of Pennsylvania, and the National Endowment for the Arts, a federal agency.

www.autumnhouse.org

For Newman, beloved on this earth

"They ask me to remember
but they want me to remember
their memories
and I keep on remembering
mine"

—Lucille Clifton

ACKNOWLEDGMENTS

Thanks very much to the editors of the following publications in which excerpts of this book first appeared, sometimes in different forms: *Atticus Review*, *Defunct*, *The Fourth River*, *Gulf Stream*, *Hippocampus*, *KGB BarLit*, *The Pittsburgh Post-Gazette*, *The Chicago Tribune*, and *Superstition Review*. Thank you to my publisher and editor Dan Cafaro, small-press champion extraordinaire. Thank you to my Pittsburgh writing family, especially Adam Matcho, Bob Pajich, and Scott Silsbe. Thank you to Erik Cirelli and Emily Rogers and Lou Ickes for always reminding me books and music, art and kindness matter. Thank you Lesley Rains, John Schulman, Kris Collins and Karen Lillis for being awesome and giving Pittsburgh books great independent homes. Thanks Lori Matcho, Paulette Poullet, and Amy Urban for your friendship and table-talk. Thank you to my students at Pitt-Greensburg and Chatham. You remind me why writing is important and keep my heart whole. Thank you to my families—the one who raised me and the ones who go on raising. Thanks to my big-hearted beautiful husband/writer Dave Newman, who makes everything possible. And thanks most of all to my son and daughter, Locklin and Phelan, who tolerate all the hours I spend moving words on a page and who remind me every day what matters more. I love you both more than anything, and more than that, and more than that.

This is primarily a work of nonfiction. Situations may have appeared in other works in different forms and different contexts. Characters are not conflated. Events may sometimes be compressed and presented out of sequence. Many names and details have been changed to protect identities. Much is based on my own memories and the narrative is faithful to my recollections. However, as a memoir in part about adoption and the fragmented life that comes from the adoption experience, this work attempts to recreate, through fiction and imagination, certain lost and key moments that affected my life, but for which I was not present. Sections titled Catholic Charities Non-Identifying Report are fictions based on facts drawn from my official adoption record. I also used stories I've been told by multiple sources and believe to be true to recreate pivotal scenes from my father's childhood.

*Belief Is Its Own
Kind of Truth,
Maybe*

I

When my real mother dies, I go looking for another one. The Catholic Charities counselor's word for this other mother I want after decades to find is biological. *Illegitimate* is another word for people who end up like me. It's what I feel now, unlawful, unauthorized, unwarranted here in this office that smells like antiseptic and rubber gloves, hot teeth drilled down to bone.

The Catholic Charities counselor has questions.

They're my questions, too.

What is the nature of your search? Why has it taken you so long?

I am nearly forty. The counselor is only slightly older, but her hair is gray and cropped like a game-show host's, like Alex Trebek's. The counselor's beige skirt hits below her knees. My mother, the mother who raised me, called this shade of beige bone. She had shoes in this color. My mother had a lot of shoes, high heels, with purses to match. She stacked them in her closet, arranged by color, white to bone to black.

"The rest of me might be going to hell," she liked to say. "But my legs are good." At 70, she'd Rockette kick and spin to show how good.

My mother and I had the same size feet, but I couldn't walk in heels. When she died, I had to decide what to do with all those beautiful shoes I couldn't bear to give away or leave at Goodwill.

It's one of the things that bothers me, the idea of strangers walking around in shoes my mother used to dance in.

The Catholic Charities woman doesn't look the dancing type. She has thick ankles. Her shoes are rubber-soled. Her hands are tight as an onion in her lap. Beneath those hands is my file, my name printed in black Sharpie on the tab. The folder looks new, even though the information inside is decades old.

"Biological," she says again, and I think of warfare, congressional panels, fear.

"I wasn't ready before," I say to the counselor.

"And now," I say, "I am."

≈ⴰⵔ⵿⵿ⵔ≈

Before *Jeopardy*, Alex Trebek hosted another game show called *To Tell the Truth*. On *To Tell the Truth*, celebrities had to sort a real news-worthy person from a panel of imposters.

Everybody lied. Everybody lied until they didn't. That was the fun, waiting for the real person to please stand up.

≈ⴰⵔ⵿⵿ⵔ≈

The Catholic Charities counselor has questions.

They're my questions, too, though until now I thought I knew the answers. Here, under interrogation, everything is suspect. Every answer becomes another question.

Who are you? Why are you here?

A silver cross glints at the counselor's throat. Her face is blank. She doesn't blink. This seems conscious, as if she wills herself not to blink, as if she believes not-blinking will make her seem open and honest and incapable of lying, even if the subject is someone's impostered life.

I hate her.

A moment later, I feel sorry.

The counselor nods. She unfolds her hands and picks up my file. She taps it once against her palm, then sets it on the far side of the desk behind a framed picture of her dog.

The dog, a white poodle, wears a birthday hat. Its front paws straddle a cake shaped like a bone.

❧

The counselor's dog looks like Tina II, the dog I had growing up. Tina II was a replacement dog, the fallback when Tina I died during surgery for something I can't remember.

"Goddamn butcher," my father said of the veterinarian, who'd offered to dispose of Tina I for a fee, no problem.

My father went to collect Tina I's body. He threatened the vet, who reimbursed the cost for the botched surgery. My father, stooped and heartsick, buried Tina I in the back yard next to my mother's tomato garden. He didn't mark the spot, no stone, no sticks, because that would make it hard to mow over.

After a while, weeks maybe, when the grass seed he sprinkled sprouted up and the weeds came back, it was hard to remember where he'd put her. After that, he took my mother and me to a poodle breeder to pick out Tina II.

Back then, age 7 or so, I was lonely and asking for a brother or a sister.

"Now even if we wanted to, how would we do that?" my mother, who couldn't have children of her own, said.

That's the phrase people used, children of her own.

I didn't think of myself as a replacement dog. I never asked my mother if she'd known if the baby she lost, the one who nearly killed her, was a boy or a girl.

"We always wanted a girl," she said, and I figured she meant me.

"Just go pick another one up from that home," I said about the brother or sister I wanted.

I imagined an orphanage was like a grocery store, all bright lights and orderly aisles, babies displayed like melons. I imagined a place where people took numbers and stood in lines.

"Be satisfied. You have us," my mother said. "That's enough."

⁓◦§◦⁓

I used to roll Tina II's ears in sponge rollers. I held her against my chest while I slept. I told her secrets and my father made her steak and dressed her in a knit sweater and booties and my mother made her a birthday cake with trick candles and Tina II stayed a dog and not a person and after a while I decided maybe everyone, no matter what, ended up alone like me.

∽⧉∾

"Your dog," I say to the counselor. "He's cute."

"Yes, well." She clears her throat and looks off somewhere above my head. "You should know there aren't any guarantees. Sometimes the stories are happy like on TV. Sometimes they're not. Most times, not."

I nod. There is a blister on the roof of my mouth. I press my tongue against it until it hurts. I press harder and try to get the blister to pop.

The counselor hands me a clipboard.

"Don't leave anything out," she says, and turns back to her computer.

Even the easiest questions seem like tricks—name, date of birth, known medical history.

The others are worse.

What is your expected outcome?

How satisfied are you with your life? Rate from 1 to 10.

Do you consider yourself stable? Content?

If you had one thing to tell your birth parent(s), what would it be?

Outside, Pittsburgh sparkles in the autumn light. All

those rivers and bridges, connecting everything to everything. In Point State Park, near the fountain, kids who should be in school are flying kites.

⋯⊰⊱⋯

Years ago, one of my high school teachers, Mr. Engle, an aging hippie with a long beard he'd braid into pigtails, encouraged romanticism. When John Lennon was shot, Mr. Engle wept in class and spent an entire period playing "Imagine" over and over on the school's beat-up record player. The record player's arm had a penny taped to the top so the needle wouldn't skip. The speaker was scratchy. Mr. Engle's eyes were red for days.

Not long after that, he gave me Thoreau's "On Civil Disobedience."

"The unexamined life isn't worth living, man," Mr. Engle said.

"If a plant cannot live according to its nature," Thoreau wrote, "it dies; and so a man."

The next week, I skipped school and caught a bus downtown. I walked to The Point and waded fully dressed into the fountain. I stood in the center and looked out through a kaleidoscope of sun and water. Off in the distance, two red inclines clamored along Mt. Washington, one on its way up and one down, the people inside waving and making faces at each other as they passed, and I felt the city inside me, one beautiful mirrored thing, a record playing over and over. Imagine. I was young and believed I knew my place in the world.

Then a security guard came and made me get out. I took the bus back to the suburbs, shivering in the air conditioning. The driver eyed me in the mirror. A lady next to me held her purse. At my stop, a man in filthy overalls who smelled like whiskey and salami got down on one knee and sang "When Irish Eyes Are Smiling." He held my sopping pant leg. He looked into my green Irish eyes that were nothing like my mother's.

"Doesn't that just break your heart," the bus driver said.

⋖⟊⟊⟊⟊⟊⟊⟊

Once, at the height of his fame, Alex Trebek shaved his trademark mustache. He wore a fake one on TV, an April Fool's joke. When he tore it off on-air and showed the world his naked face, it made news. Major networks tracked the evolution of Alex Trebek's mustache with photo essays, stock footage. Fans grieved.

"I just felt like it," Trebek said about shaving. "And it got so much press I couldn't believe it. The wars with Iraq or whatever, and people are all in a stew over my moustache. Get a life."

When he grew his mustache back, my mother, who loved *Jeopardy*, said, "Thank god. He looks like himself."

⋖⟊⟊⟊⟊⟊⟊⟊

"You are what people think you are," my mother liked to say, as if everything came down to perception, as if there were no such thing as a true self.

9

Back to the questionnaire.

I fill it with lies. I rate my life a 9. I write, "I see life as an opportunity for growth."

Was I content? Yes. Stable? Yes.

What is your expected outcome?

What one thing would you tell your birth parent(s)?

I write: "I'd like a medical history."

I write: "I'm happy."

These are, I know, good answers.

2

The house is empty when I get home from Catholic Charities. My husband has taken the kids out, to the city park probably. Our son, Locklin, likes to play in the rock piles underneath the Panther Hollow Bridge.

On one side of the bridge, there's a remnant of a one-story-tall, graffiti'd face of Andre the Giant. Andre's eyes, stenciled, blackened, painted over and dissolving in light, look even sadder than they did on TV. In life, in death, in cartoons, he always seems to be melting and on the verge of tears.

As a kid I watched Andre the Giant take down bad guys—George the Animal Steel, the Iron Sheik, various Russians. My father, who was rarely happy, liked to watch wrestling, the spectacle of it, the clear and simple lines, the way it was nothing like life.

"You can always tell the bastards from the rest," my father would say, and it was almost always true, except for Andre.

"A change of heart," Vince McMahon said when the gentle giant of the 1970s became a villain ten years later. Hulk Hogan in his red-white-and-blue Speedo needed someone to bump against. The world was short on bad guys with Eastern European accents. The Berlin Wall had come down. Andre the Giant would do.

When the crowd called for blood, they got it. A chair to a head, a face ground into the ropes, skin sanded to pulp, a red trail along the mat.

"You never can tell about people."

My father said that, too.

⚬❁⚬

My son, Locklin, is three, going on four. He likes *Star Wars*: good guys in white, bad guys in black. The Force. The Dark Side. Locklin has a collection of toy light sabers —blue for good guys, red for bad guys, green for guys who feel conflicted.

Before trips to the park, my husband loads a back-pack with sabers. When he and Locklin go alone, they have long battles to the tops of the rock piles. They knock each other down and come home filthy, tiny stones in their shoes, rock shards embedded in their skin, dirt ground into their underwear.

Today, though, they won't be alone. Locklin will have to climb solo while his father and sister urge him on. He'll slash the air around him. He'll imagine himself surrounded. He'll imagine the many ways he will or will not pull this off.

Phelan, our daughter, will be in a backpack. She'll hold onto my husband's hair, tiny fingers digging in at the roots, drool dripping into his ears, the babbling cadence of her small voice. "Such a happy baby," people at the grocery always say, and it's true. My son, with his green saber, his darker, more complicated moods, takes after me. My daughter is more like my husband, so much pure light.

Phelan is four months old. I was pregnant with her when my mother died. I didn't know this then. If I had, maybe it would have made a difference. If my mother knew she would soon have a granddaughter, maybe she would have tried harder to stay alive. "Something to live for," people say, but my mother had much to live for already—a grandson, a nice son-in-law who cut her grass and liked her meatballs and listened to her stories.

She had me.

"I need you," I told my mother in the hospital.

"I'm tired," she said.

She said, "No. You don't."

By 40, I'd finally pulled the strings of my life together into something that looked like it would hold. What my mother meant—I had a good husband. A son. A steady job teaching writing at a university. A life.

"I was 40. Then I was fortier," a friend wrote.

I'm fortier.

I can't imagine when I will ever be old enough to stop being my mother's daughter.

I can't imagine when I will ever stop needing her.

~⊰⊱~

Phelan isn't named after my mother. She has my birth name, a last name for a first name. I thought it was pretty.

I thought it made sense. My daughter has my husband's personality, but she looks so much like me. We have the same blonde hair, same green eyes. One day soon she'll insist my baby pictures are her baby pictures.

I thought giving her that name was a way to honor roots.

I always pronounce Phelan as Fay-Lynn.

This is my daughter's name.

At Catholic Charities, they said I had it wrong.

"The family says it Fee-Lynn," the counselor with the bone shoes told me. She didn't look up from the forms I'd filled out, the ones she was examining for errors.

Fee-Lynn.

It's not nearly as nice.

⋞⟨⟩⋟

I should have named my daughter for my mother, my real mother, though my mother hated her name and wouldn't have wanted me to pass it on.

"It's an old lady's name," she said.

My mother's name was Alberta. She shortened it to Bertie, but it still made her wince. Her maiden name was Bonde, switched from the Italian Bondi with an "i" so it would seem more American. My grandmother's name was Ethel. Ethel, out of spite my mother believed, named her children as follows: Florence, Velma, Gertrude, Alberta, and August.

"One name more hideous than the next," my mother said.

Most were named for friends, except for August, who was named for his father and made everyone call him Butch.

My grandfather, August Bondi, was an orphan, too. His mother delivered him to an orphanage one day when he was nine or ten. She packed a small suitcase. Clothes, a child's Bible. It was the beginning of the Depression. She said she couldn't afford to feed him. She said he was difficult. She didn't say she drank too much. She didn't say she wanted her own life.

My mother said her father wouldn't talk about it. She said he always made sure they had plenty to eat, even ice cream, three or four different flavors, gallon cartons lined up in the ice box when there wasn't money for anything else.

I never knew my grandfather. I know he made bathtub gin to pay for food. I know a few pictures—a thin man, sad eyes like Andre the Giant's, mugging a tough-guy stance, paperboy cap down low, one pin-striped leg cocked on the fender of a black Ford. I know he died on his birthday the year I was born.

"He would have loved you," my mother always said.

Maybe I would have loved him back.

Two orphans.

How a mother could take her child by the hand and give him over to strangers, how she could walk away and not look back, I don't know. I don't know what she told him, what she could possibly have told him, to make him stay and believe, in what?

That she'd come back.

That she wouldn't come back.

That his life would be better either way.

⋘⋙

Or I do know. Motherhood is a conflicted state, not clear and simple at all. Very few mothers are monsters.

Joan Crawford, maybe.

⋘⋙

"You're a good mother," my mother told me the day I was weeping in her driveway.

Locklin was very young then, a year or so. I'd gone to the grocery store. He screamed the whole time. He thrashed and wailed and I had to hold my hands over his hands in the cart to keep him still. He was a beautiful baby, but he cried so much and so long that I started crying, too. I cried over bills and junk mail and *Mister Rogers' Neighborhood*. I cried over Oreo commercials, where fathers taught their children how to pull apart and dunk a cookie and scrape the icing off with their teeth. I cried in class, when I tried to explain to my students about the writer Raymond Carver, how, when a doctor told him he had cancer and would die, Carver thanked the doctor, "habit being so strong." I cried that day in my mother's driveway when the grocery bag tore open and milk spilled and flooded the trunk.

I knew no matter how I tried to clean it up, the milk would molder and stink and the car already smelled. It smelled like wet diapers and diaper powder and Butt Paste, a brown muddy-spearmint diaper-rash lotion, the only thing that worked. The car smelled like shit and carsick puke and the lingering grease from the fast food I ate because I was too tired to cook or eat anything else. I smelled like all those things, too, all the time. I smelled feral, animal, desperate, everything I was.

"You're a good mother," my mother said, a gift, a mantra, a promise, like something she'd said to herself through the years.

She tried to help me, but I kept on crying like the child I was. My mother sopped up milk and sprayed the car with air freshener and took my son from his car seat and rocked and rocked and rocked him until he passed out, which is what he did instead of falling asleep. He never just fell asleep peacefully, like babies in commercials. My son passed out from exhaustion, all that anger, all those built-up then let-go tears.

3

Back from Catholic Charities in this empty house, I make coffee. I take my time. I grind the beans and heat the milk and linger in the kitchen. I look out the window over the sink, where my mother's lilac bush is blooming. I think about going out to clip some blossoms to bring inside, the way my mother used to, but I don't because lilac makes everyone in my own family sneeze.

Instead I go check my e-mail. There's a new message.

The Subject is "Amelia Phelan," my birth name. The message reads: "I am your sister."

There's a phone number.

I print the message. Then I call Catholic Charities. My hands shake. I do what I always do when I'm terrified. I make a joke.

"I always heard you guys were better than the mob at finding people, but this is amazing," I say to the bone-shoe counselor who is so silent I can't hear her breathe.

I tell her about the message. She doesn't say anything. I hear paper shuffling.

I say, "That's amazing." I say, "Really."

I say, "How did you manage this so fast?" and she says, "We didn't."

The woman who calls herself my sister is Blonde4Eva. This is her e-mail address. I find this upsetting, even though I've dyed my hair blonde for years. "I've always been a natural blonde," I say, meaning I dye my hair to match my baby pictures.

"What do you think it means?" I ask my husband, who shakes his head. My husband says I shouldn't judge people by their e-mail addresses.

Fluffykitty1000. Poetgrrrl. Flyguy. Blonde4Eva.

"It doesn't mean anything," my husband says.

The Catholic Charities counselor has promised to be in touch. She wants to contact the birth family. "I have to advise you to not continue this correspondence until we speak with the birth family," the counselor says. "Until then, we can neither confirm nor deny that this woman is or is not who she says she is."

"From mobster to politician," I say.

"What?" she says.

"Thank you," I say, "I will."

Blonde4Eva sends more messages. I read them over and over. They're a puzzle, pieces of sky that don't fit. I've loved words so deeply and for so long I thought it was genetic. But Blonde4Eva struggles with grammar, syntax.

"I'm not judging," I tell my husband, though of course I am.

It's a shitty thing to do.

≈⊙|৯≈

I'm a writer. My friend Patience is a librarian. We both judge people on their words, the books they love, if they own book shelves, whether or not they love books at all. Sometimes we feel bad, but we go on doing it, the way people on Wall Street judge people on their stock portfolios and plumbers judge people on how they feel about copper pipe and my mother judged people by whether or not they could twirl spaghetti on a fork without using a spoon.

Everybody needs a compass in this world.

≈⊙|৯≈

"I all ways KNEW," Blonde4Eva writes.

Two words. All. Ways.

KNEW in capital letters, bold type. Green and highlighted.

"Decoding," I tell my husband when he asks what I'm doing now.

≈⊙|৯≈

Patience and I did not grow up in families of readers. In our craggy Pennsylvania towns, it was better to be caught with a cigarette than a book. It was better for our mothers to catch us getting fingered by a boy than catch us on the couch reading.

Reading was uppity.

Reading made people think things.

"Devil's work," Patience's mother would say.

My mother called it lazy.

"Don't you have something useful to do?" she'd say, and mean dishes.

In Patience's house, there was a Bible and copies of *Highlights for Children* lifted from the dentist's office. There was *The Farmer's Almanac*. There was *TV Guide*.

Me, I kept a Webster's dictionary in the bathroom of my parents' pink one-story house. I hid it under the sink, behind stacks of toilet paper and my father's tubes of Preparation H. The dictionary's cover was denim blue, designed to look like the back pocket of a pair of jeans, an everyday thing.

My mother hated bathroom reading most of all.

"Shit or get off the pot," she'd say.

"The mouth on that one," my father, the mill worker, said when they fought. "Just like her mother."

≈⊰⊱≈

I saw words as handed-down things, like heart disease and bad teeth.

Orphaned, adopted, I was not my parents' child.

≈⊰⊱≈

Blonde4Eva writes: "My mother was born of two Irish imagrants. And I suppose no I know that things were no good. We have 3 other siblings."

22

Stet—the word editors use when they don't correct errors because the error means something more. An error can be an insight. An error can be a map. Stet means "let it stand."

When he was President of the United States, George Bush misspoke a lot. "I'm the decider," he said, and journalists left his mistakes alone.

"I'll be long gone before some smart person ever figures out what happened inside this Oval Office," George Bush said.

"Terrorists have no disregard for human life," George Bush said.

"Amigo! Amigo!" George Bush called out to Italian Prime Minister Silvio Berlusconi as the cameras rolled.

⤳⟨⟩⤲

Growing up, I'd hide in the bathroom and read and memorize dictionary pages. I'd find smug new words and use them in sentences at dinner.

Words I liked: Flibbertigibbet. Oxymoron. Loquacious.

"I could wipe my ass with what you know," my father liked to say.

"I don't know where you came from," my mother would say, and I'd say, "Neither do I."

⤳⟨⟩⤲

"I don't know where you came from," Patience's mother would say to her, too, though Patience was what my grandmother called a natural-born child.

I was not natural-born.

I was loved, mostly, despite it.

❧

With Blonde4Eva, it isn't just the grammar.

It's the implied sense of drama—"I suppose no I know."

I ask my husband again about the meaning.

"What do *you* think it means?" my husband asks back, and I don't answer.

❧

One time my father bought a set of encyclopedias from a man who was selling them door-to-door. My father never opened the door for strangers, but this time he did. I don't know why. The set was *The World Book of Knowledge*. The books looked like bibles, egg-shell colored covers, gold spines, gold-tipped pages with strings sewn into the binding to use as bookmarks.

"She's smart," my father would say to explain why I'd hole up for hours reading A-C when my mother thought I should be outside playing.

"She'll ruin her eyes," my mother said.

"She'll go to college," my father said. "She'll meet a good man."

My father bought a bookshelf, the only one in the house, a low two-shelved number he put together just for the encyclopedias. The bookshelf had a glass door that slid closed to keep the books safe from dust.

My father wanted the books safe.

My mother wanted me safe from the books.

"I want what's mine to stay mine," my mother liked to say, something she learned from her father, the orphan who would have loved me. He meant he wanted his children close. He meant he didn't want anyone to leave him ever again.

"She'll get ideas," my mother would say about the encyclopedias and mean the world. She sighed a lot. She dusted the bookshelf with a pink feather duster.

As far as I knew, she never opened any of the books.

⋖⟨│⟩⋗

Patience and I met in college. We were English majors. I wanted to be a journalist. "Pipe dream," my mother said, and I imagined a pipe as big as a factory, an assembly-line of clouds. To be cruel, my mother told people I was studying to be Barbara Walters.

I'm not sure how Patience's mother explained things.

⋖⟨│⟩⋗

When Patience was eight, an encyclopedia salesman came to her house, too. Albion, Pennsylvania was farm country, tornado country, the 1970s, the kind of place where people name their children after virtues or deserts or saints. There were a lot of girls named Hope and Mary and one girl named Sahara. The day of the encyclopedia, the doorbell rang. Patience's mother, expecting vacuum cleaners or a new kind of floor soap, opened the door, and this man dressed for the city said, "Might I borrow a few moments of your time, Miss?"

Patience's mother looked more than her age.

She looked like a woman with housecoats and three children and a life in Albion, Pennsylvania. She looked like a woman who'd welcome the opportunity to purchase a new kind of floor soap and she knew it.

The man held up a big white book. The words *Wonderland of Knowledge* were embossed in gold on the cover and there was a picture of a globe, shiny blue for water, more gold for the land.

Patience peeked from behind her mother.

The man bent down. "Hello, honey," he said. "Do you like to read? I know I do."

Patience liked to read. Patience liked globes, too.

The man made a flourish, a magic trick. He tried to present the book to Patience's mother, who kept both hands on the doorframe.

"You'll be giving your beautiful daughter a head start," he said. "She'll have an advantage over other kids."

The *TV Guide* was open on the coffee table, dog-eared, highlighted. Patience's mother was proud of their TV, the sturdiest piece of furniture in the house. "This will outlast me," she'd say, and pat the TV like a puppy.

The salesman held his magic book like a lantern. Patience watched her mother once-over his shined shoes, tweed pants, smooth hands, gold watch big as a compass.

"Now why," Patience's mother said, the words slow, clicking like deadbolts, "would my daughter deserve an advantage over anyone?"

⋞◦⫯◦⋟

Patience took care of both her parents until they died. Now she lives in a small apartment with a cat and many books, and says she doesn't like people though both of us know it's not true. Patience's car is filled with books on tape. When she drives, she turns up the volume and likes to feel the stories, those other worlds whirling inside her.

⋞◦⫯◦⋟

Blonde4Eva says she found out about me two years ago.

"One of my cousins dropped the bomb on me," she writes.

She says her mother denied then admitted it.

Her mother gave her few details.

"Were you born with a club foot?" Blonde4Eva wants to know, and I want to tell her no, I was born with two, two clubbed feet.

⋞◦⫯◦⋟

When my friend Sam first found her birth mother, her birth mother sent a lot of letters. The letters were written on stationery, parchment-ish paper with butterflies skit-

27

tering around the scalloped edges. This bothered Sam a lot. Sam dyes her hair blue and keeps it shorn a half inch all around. She wears black biker jackets. She wears serious black glasses. She writes poems about Sid Vicious and Wu Tang and fuck the police.

"This cannot be my mother," she'd say and wave the letters in the air like surrender.

The writing on the letters was off, too. Big loopy script. Bubble-dotted i's. Lots of talk about God and how much Sam's mother relied on Him at times like these.

Praise God. God willing. God forgive me. God forgive you.

"I'll pray for you," my birth mother will write to me very soon.

It will be the most awful thing she does until she does something worse.

⊰⊱

I wonder if my story, the one my parents told me and the one I helped invent, has been wrong from the start.

"You are probably as weary as I, to determine the truth so that nobody gets hurt," Blonde4Eva writes.

There are so many versions of the truth.

All of them would hurt someone, I think.

⊰⊱

Blonde4Eva writes: "If it turns out that you are not the same child you are definitely close to finding out who is."

28

"Do you want a sandwich?" my husband asks from the kitchen. I can see him in there, eating cheese from the bag, a stack of buns on the cutting board.

I know he wants me to come in and help, fry some lunch meat in a pan.

"Eat something," he says, like he's my mother.

4

I fell asleep on the couch and stayed there. Now it's 5 a.m. and Locklin's awake. He pries my fingers open like latches on a gate. I sleep fetal, hands balled into fists. My fingers are sore from the strain, like I've been punching someone. Locklin's face is inches from mine. His breath smells like chocolate milk and sleep. I squint awake as he presses a doll into my hand.

"Be him," my son orders.

The lines of light from the window blinds make my son's face look caged.

It's what I feel, too.

Somehow, Locklin's dragged the plastic toy bin across the room. He's dumped everything onto the floor, and my first thought is I'll have to clean it up. I'll have to get off this couch and clean and how could I possibly be expected do that now.

Over on the table, the computer screen is blinking. It's an Apple computer, shiny and sports-car red. It looks like a toy. I wonder about Blonde4Eva, her e-mail, so intimate and impersonal all at once.

"We can neither confirm nor deny," the Catholic Charities counselor said.

I close my eyes again.

My son's hard little finger pokes my cheek, like he's testing a cake.

"Be him," Locklin says.

The last time my husband fell asleep on the couch like this and tried to brush Locklin off, Locklin crumbled Cocoa Pebbles cereal and sprinkled it on my husband's face until he woke up, furious, choking, chocolaty rice flakes in his nose and eyelashes. It was 5 a.m. then, too.

"Done sleeping," Locklin said, to explain things.

"Who does something like that?" my husband, swatting, squinting, half-blind from cereal dust, asked our son, who looked confused.

Now Locklin tries to grab my eyelashes and pull one of my eyes open.

"Puppets," Locklin says, which is what he calls this game, one of his favorites.

This early in the morning, I dread it.

Toppled from the toy bin, there's a huge collection of stuffed animals, action figures and dolls. Locklin calls all of them puppets. When he says "be him," he means method acting. He means "once more, with feeling."

Some puppets are easier than others—Elmo, that helium squeal, the ratcheted maniacal giggle; Animal from The Muppets, *manamana*. But this doll in my hands is another thing. He's anonymous, non-descript. He looks like a prince, maybe, or a good pirate. I don't recognize him from any movie. His jaw is sharp enough to clean fingernails. His eyes are very blue. He's blonde, which is what my son calls him, Blondie.

Blondie.

Blonde4Eva.

It will take me a while to see and appreciate the irony.

"Be Blondie," Locklin commands.

I try and always fail.

My son has invented an entire life for Blondie, but no one knows what that life is because Locklin won't explain it. There's no way to know what he thinks Blondie should sound like. There's no way to guess the role he's mapped out for Blondie in his mind.

Locklin shakes his head and says again, "Be him," but I don't know the lines. I don't know the gestures. I'm supposed to understand—through osmosis, maybe—Blondie's life story channeling through his tan plastic skin into mine.

⋘⟨⟩⋙

Growing up, I had fantasies about a sister. She'd show up on the porch, drooping blonde pigtails, banged-up suitcase, a note from the adoption agency. We'd be best and instant friends. We'd do each other's hair. We'd side against my parents, who'd become our parents, who'd become strangers who could never understand us.

Two castaways. Two lost princesses. Two beautiful lonely girls, one pink, one blue, like the two girls in the kitschy paintings my mother bought at Woolworth's and hung over the couch. Two sad-eyed moppets with mandolins at their feet, waiting for something.

My imagined sister and I, we'd stay up late, reading,

flashlights under our covers, matching shadows showing through the sheets. My sister would be kind, like the
mother who'd given us both up even though we knew she
didn't want to, even though she loved us very much, even
though one day she'd come back.

"Hope to hear from you," Blonde4Eva writes.

"Be him," my son says now about Blondie.

I try a generic Disney swagger, a low-voiced "hi there."

"No," my son says, and he looks like he might cry, he's
that disappointed, distressed. He takes Blondie out of my
hand and dances him against my cheek. "Be him."

But I don't know how.

I don't know who he could possibly be.

5

Blonde4Eva sends me a link, a Phelan family website. On the site, there are pictures, a family tree, a cartoon drawing of an actual tree. Names form in columns. Family history. A list of famous Phelans. "Bardic clan. Royal lineage," the site explains. We include—they include?—writers, musicians, career criminals.

"Phelan comes from O'Failain. It means 'of the wolf,'" my friend Sinead, who's from Galway, tells me.

Years ago, in Galway and throughout Ireland, homes for unwed mothers and their children were called Magdalene homes. "For the fallen women," Sinead says, and lowers her voice like she's talking about cancer.

Galway's Magdalene home was called Tuam. It was run by nuns, the Bon Secours sisters. Bon Secours means good help. "Good help to those in need," was the home's motto. The unwed mothers in Tuam worked two years' hard labor with no pay to atone for their sins. Their children were taken from them.

Illegitimates, the nuns of Tuam called them.

Many illegitimates died in Tuam, unwanted bodies buried in unmarked graves in the yard.

"Your lucky," Blonde4Eva writes. "You don't know."

⚬⊰⊱⚬

Sinead is an accountant. When I lived in New York, we were housemates. There were seven of us in a house, six Irish accountants and me. We took turns making dinner. My housemates knew how to make only one thing—spaghetti Bolognese. Ragu spaghetti sauce. Ground meat. So it was six days of spaghetti Bolognese, and one day of me making something no one else wanted to eat.

"I'm Irish, too," I told my housemates when I first moved in.

"No," Sinead said, "you're American," but she was gentle about it.

⚬⊰⊱⚬

It's easy to spot an American, Sinead says. It's in the body language.

"Americans take up so much space," she says, and points out a man on the subway, his knees spread wide, a brown bag on the orange seat beside him. His *Times* is accordion-folded, proper subway etiquette, but his elbows flare like peacocks.

"It's like they're trying to take in the world," Sinead says, as if I wasn't one of them after all.

⚬⊰⊱⚬

I don't have the world inside me. I'm not Irish. I'm not German or Jewish, though my parents said my birth father was. I'm not Polish like my father, or Italian and Slovak like my mother. Until I married and had children, I was single, solitary, someone who most days wanted to take up no space at all.

❧

Years ago, when I was working as a journalist, I met Alex Haley, the author of *Roots*. He was kind, gentle with a nervous young reporter sent to interview one of her idols. When I stumbled, he asked me questions about my writing, about school, my own family history. I told him I didn't have a family history, not really, and he said, "That's its own kind of story, then." I didn't ask, but I wanted to know—if stories start at the beginning and you don't have a beginning, how do you know where the real story starts?

❧

After she moved back to Galway, Sinead found an image of the Phelan family crest and sent it to me Air Mail. The crest was printed on a beer coaster. It was green and gold, a blue line of diamonds in a diagonal slash through the middle. A sticker on a cork circle.

The crest is on the website, too. I think I should feel some deep connection to this crest, to Blonde4Eva, or to both, but I don't. I want to. I want to feel something I can't name.

"Desire drives narrative," the writers say. Desire keeps a story moving forward. Desire is the story. Sometimes a story is more than a story. Sometimes a story is a life.

✖

Tuam, Galway's Magdalene home, closed before I was born.

It will be in the news many years later for its unspeakable cruelty.

Blonde4Eva says when her grandparents left Galway, they brought the old country with them. She says her mother was raised that way.

"Very proud Irish," she writes. "Catholic."

All those lost women and children.

All those tiny unnamed bones.

✖

Blonde4Eva sends more e-mails—a cousin with breast cancer, a steelworker grandfather who lost a leg, her mother's throat cancer and the hole in her neck she talks and breathes through.

"Froggy but she does alright."

Blonde4Eva says her mother can't give up smoking even now. Blonde4Eva says her mother holds a cigarette to the hole in her neck to let the smoke in.

✖

My mother, the mother who raised me, smoked. Young, dark-haired, a Kool menthol seesawing between her fingers, glamorous as any movie star. She could blow smoke through her nose. She could blow smoke rings, tiny life preservers lifting off from her pink-glossed lips.

"My magic trick," she called it.

∽⸙∾

"Stubborn," Blonde4Eva says about her mother. "Old school."

Blonde4Eva says she herself was born lazy-eyed. People thought she wasn't smart. She says she's never recovered from this.

"I am smart," she says, "They don't know."

∽⸙∾

"This one's smart," my father told everyone about me when I was still a baby. "I can see it in her eyes. This one's no dummy." He wanted me to go to college, made sure I went to college. "To meet a better class of men," he said.

My first word after daddy and hi was *circus*.

"I thought you'd never say mommy," my mother said.

∽⸙∾

Blonde4Eva highlights her text in lime green. It's hard to read. She uses a lot of capital letters.

"Don't shout," I read once in a guide to e-mail etiquette.

Blonde4Eva says she's always had a feeling about me.

I was something missing.

"I KNEW," she says, and repeats it.

All that green.

She says it was hard for her growing up. Poor. Rough
neighborhood.

She says I should be grateful, something I've heard
all my life.

You should be grateful your parents took you out of
that orphanage.

You wouldn't be able to walk if your parents never
took you out of that orphanage.

You should get down on your knees and thank god
you have food and clothes and parents who took you out
of that orphanage.

You should be grateful.

Who knows how you would have ended up?

~⸙~

Blonde4Eva says, "Listen."

She says her mother is strange about strangers. She
says she could maybe set up a meeting. She says I should
trust her to handle things.

She says everything will be better now that she's
found me.

6

Phelan, my daughter, wears a leg brace. She has problems with her hip. The brace keeps her legs apart, divided into two parentheses, like she's always on a horse. It's hard to hold her close. When I rock her before bed, I take her out of the brace, even though I'm not supposed to do this. I rub her legs and feel her skin on my skin. I think the brace hurts her, but she's such a happy baby, always smiling.

I worry that the problem will spread, that she'll be like me, with my two clubbed feet, my crooked legs, in casts up to my hips for years. All those surgeries. This is what I told the counselor at Catholic Charities. "I need a medical history," I said. "For my kids."

"Hereditary, yes," Phelan's doctor says about the hip, "but don't worry, Mom. She's not like you." The doctor is Polish. He has the same accent my father worked hard to hide. He wears gold chains, big rings. A pendant of an eagle peeks out from his scrubs. His scrubs are blue, the same color as his eyes. He wears clogs, white ones, very expensive and European looking.

The day he diagnosed Phelan, the doctor flirted with the pretty nurse who came in to strap my daughter into the brace. "Ah, here she is, my beautiful assistant," he said, and the nurse blushed. Phelan cried. Wailed. The nurse wore pink scrubs with smiley faces poxed all over them. She didn't seem to notice Phelan's crying. She stuffed Phelan's legs into the brace, one then the other, two bread loaves, and pulled the Velcro straps tight, the sound of tearing.

The nurse said, "Oh doctor," like she was a character on TV.

❧

It's Halloween. My son is dressed as Spiderman. His costume has built-in muscles, all padded biceps and abs. "Twip," he says as he swings by, shooting invisible webs between us.

"How does it feel?" my friend Sam, the adopted one with the butterfly-stationery birth mother, asked once.

She'd run into Locklin and me at the mall. I didn't know what she meant at first. Locklin had been grumpy. He was very small then, and I carried him in a Baby Bjorn pack across my chest. He'd finally drifted off to sleep when Sam saw us pacing back and forth in front of The Gap. We must have looked peaceful, but there was dried milk on my clothes, baby spit in my hair, what felt like a dampening diaper against my belly. Underneath the Baby Bjorn, Locklin jabbed my ribs with his fists. I was terrified he'd wake up.

"To have, you know, that connection," she said. "Blood."

It sounded romantic, magical. A blood connection. My first. My only.

And it was.

And it wasn't.

I looked past Sam to the headless denimed mannequins in the Gap's window, their elbows cranked like contortionists, hands palms up. I said, "Good." I said, "I'm tired a lot."

Sam is a poet. I know she wanted something better than that. But even now, I can't think of the right, more profound thing to say.

I love my children.

My children have so many needs, all of them bigger than my own.

"I know I could never do it," Sam said about children, almost a boast, the way lots of people do. When they say, "I could never," they mean "how could you." When they say, "I could never," they look at a dried puke-smear and think, "thank god." When Sam talks about her adoption, she calls it the severing, the primal wound. She calls blood red sugar.

"Twip," Locklin says. He holds both hands palm out to shoot his webs, like he's offering me everything he has.

All those threads between us that can't be cut.

⋙⟨⟩⋘

Lately, even out of costume, Locklin's taken on an alter-ego. He calls himself HS, Human Spider. We let him draw the letters on a red turtleneck. When he wears it, he pulls the turtleneck up over his nose, with only his eyes showing.

On the fridge, there's a self-portrait he's made of himself as HS. Beneath the drawing—a good likeness, all wide-eyed and spike-haired—he's written the word *Helps*.

My husband spelled it out, but Locklin wrote it himself, the letters shaky but insistent.

"I'll save you," he says, and swoops into the room.

❦

Phelan can't wear the costume I bought her, a fuzzy Winnie-the-Pooh. It won't fit over her brace. I bought it because of the mobile that spirals over her crib, tiny Pooh bears chasing jars of honey, a kind of baby Grecian Urn thing. She reaches for the bears, giggles, tries to kick her legs up and out of the brace to get at them. The mobile is the first thing she's ever loved.

It's ridiculous, but I cry over the costume. I save it in a box in the closet, I don't know why, and cry the whole way to Target, where I'll buy her another costume, a lady bug.

The lady bug costume is o.k.—a sack, open at the bottom, enough room for her brace and spread legs. It comes with fuzzy red and black socks, and a pair of pompom antennae strapped to a headband. I'll carry Phelan door-to-door for trick-or-treating. I'll carry her past the judges' stand at the town Halloween parade, where she'll win $5 for cutest costume.

"Cute as a bug," one judge will say.

I'll carry her the way my parents carried me, though

44

they did it for years, with both my legs in casts. They talked about the bruises they had, strings of them around their waists and thighs, from where I bounced and banged my casts, eager to get down and walk.

Back home, my husband snaps pictures, Phelan flat on her back in the lady bug sack. Her eyes cross when she tries to focus on the antennae that flop over her forehead.

She looks confused.

7

The Catholic Charities counselor calls. She says she has been in touch with the birth mother. The birth mother refuses everything—a meeting, a medical history, correspondence of any kind. The birth mother wants no contact. The birth mother believed the records were permanently sealed. The birth mother wants the records permanently sealed.

The birth mother is immoveable on these points.

This is the word the counselor uses, immoveable.

The counselor does not say "your birth mother." She does not use the birth mother's name, which, unspoken, feels forbidden, as if I should forget everything I already know, as if this phone call has the power to make that happen.

I am standing in my real mother's kitchen when this call comes in. I am leaning over my mother's sink, where she leaned and did dishes and filled my father's coffee pot with water. I am looking out at my mother's lilacs again, and at her flowering dogwood, her most prized tree, grown from a sapling, kept safe from my father's mower for years.

The dogwood is blooming, its white petals spotted with red, another cluster of deeper red in the centers. My mother, Catholic, believed the stories—Christ crucified on a cross made from dogwood, the tree's growth stunted in retribution for eternity, the flowers mapping his wounds, the red center a crown of thorns.

"Dogwoods are hard to grow," my mother always said, proud of her care and skill, proud this one survived.

I don't think it's true—dogwoods are everywhere—but belief is its own kind of truth, maybe.

"The birth mother has health issues," the counselor says, and mentions the throat cancer, a voice box partially removed. "Still," the counselor says, "she was *quite* spirited."

And then the counselor does something I didn't think possible. This woman, with her bone shoes and clothes, her office of files and clipboards, her dog with its bone-shaped birthday cake, laughs. She laughs so hard she has to pull the phone back for few seconds—I hear it, the distance—to try to get her balance. It doesn't help.

"I have to say, she really gave me a go," the counselor says. "Swore at me up and down. She screamed at me, I mean screamed. No voice box and all. Imagine!"

The counselor says, "That's never happened to me."

The counselor says, "Not in all my years of doing this."

The counselor says, "Sometimes it doesn't go well, but never like this."

She stops finally, catches herself, pulls her laugh back in. She says, "Well then." She clears her throat, says, "I wish I had better news."

She says, "I'm here if you need to talk."

I mention Blonde4Eva, and she says, "I can't discuss that per the birth mother's wishes."

She says, "We have to honor the birth mother's wishes. I'm sure you understand."

She says, "I really am sorry."

I say thank you. I say I know. I say I understand.

None of this is true.

◦⊰⊱◦

When I hang up the phone, I get down on the floor and wedge myself between the kitchen cabinets. I'm alone in the house, no one to scare, and so I let it out.

I cry so hard I scare myself.

The sounds coming out of me feel distant, foreign, like the time at the dentist when, out of nowhere, he snapped my front tooth in half. The dentist had been drilling, scraping off bonding on the tooth, and the tooth cracked.

"Oh dear," the dentist said, what no one ever wants to hear a dentist say. He held up a mirror to show me what happened, the black space where my tooth had been, a jagged edge sticking out from the gum line, blood starting to pool in the edges.

I didn't recognize my face. I felt sick. I made a sound I couldn't duplicate again. It was an animal sound. Loss. Revulsion.

The sound I make today is worse than that.

About the birth mother: I had no idea I cared so much.

8

ॐ

A few days pass and we're out of batteries. Locklin drags
a toy cash register and drops it at my feet. It won't light.
The cash drawer won't open. The tiny microphone that
Locklin uses to shout "Clean up, aisle seven!" won't work.

I pop open the Emergency Preparedness Kit I bought
in a post-9/11 panic and keep stashed under the sink. I
take out two pocket flashlights and pop the batteries, then
load them into the cash register.

"That should hold you," I tell my son, as he pings the
cash register door open and closed.

We're out of other things, too—toilet paper, coffee,
and soda. We're out of baby wipes. We're down to two
diapers. Locklin needs new socks. When I realize there's
no way around it, I change Phelan's diaper and bundle
her in a plush pink baby sack—a hoodie dress with elastic
at the bottom to fit over her brace. I grab her blanket and
squeaky caterpillar, her bottle and pacifier, her diaper
bag and hippo rattle, an extra change of clothes.

There's so much gear to gather for even the smallest
errand, some days I can't face it, but today it will be good
to get out of the house, away from the phone, the computer, the mailbox.

"We'll forward a full report," the Catholic Charities counselor had said. "The report will include all non-identifying information from your file."

Locklin leans over the cash register's tiny microphone. "Mom," he says, all giggles and static. "Mommy. Mom. Mum-mum-mum-mum."

I imagine my file, redacted by the CIA, thick black lines blotting out names, dates, facts, acts to be accounted for, people to be held accountable. I can't imagine what's left to know.

"Are you o.k. with this?" my husband asks, and I say I'm fine, no worries.

My husband has two blue mugs of tea, one in each hand, and a bagel on a plate balanced over one of the mugs. He's dressed for his basement office—knit cap, slippers, cut-off sweatpants with a book tucked into the waistband. My husband's a writer, like me, when the world will let him work. Today he's supposed to be writing. I'm supposed to keep the kids away. Tomorrow he'll do the same for me. This is how we love each other.

Locklin blows into the cash register microphone. He says, "Dad. Daddy. DaDaDaDa." He says, "Cha-ching."

"She could at least have given a medical history," I say, adjusting Phelan's brace under the dress.

Phelan squirms and giggles and tries to grab my necklace, a silver heart locket that I'd given my mother years ago for Mother's Day. When my mother wore it, there were pictures of me inside. Now there are pictures of Locklin and Phelan taken right after they were born. He's wrapped in a blue blanket with teddy bears on it.

She's wrapped in a pink blanket covered with flowers. Otherwise, they look exactly the same.

"What kind of person won't give a medical history?" I say, and rub my daughter's chubby calves between my hands. "What would that hurt?"

The pictures in the locket are the size of my pinkie nails. Locklin loves for me to open the heart to show them to him.

"You're always in my heart," I tell him, and he laughs. It's what my mother used to say to me when she'd snap the heart open and closed. "Get it?" she'd say.

❦

Since the Catholic Charities call, I think about my mother a lot. I think about her as she was, but bigger, like death has turned her into a Hemingway character, smoke and hips, one tough broad.

I think about Hemingway a lot, too, all that grace under pressure. "It's awfully easy to be hardboiled about things during the daytime," Hemingway said, "but at night it's another matter."

At night I lie and wait for my husband to go to sleep. We sleep close, his right leg clamped over both of my legs, my right arm over his chest. I like to sleep like this because I want to make sure he's breathing. He snores and sometimes his breath catches and I nudge him to get it going again. Some nights I stay up late just listening to him breathe.

Then I go in and check Locklin and Phelan and make

sure they're breathing, too. I check the smoke detectors.
I check the dials on the stove. I check the door locks, the
window locks. I do this over and over again.

"I'm tired a lot," I'd told my friend Sam about motherhood.

◦◦◦

When I was very young, I told my parents I loved them
all the time. "Pass the salt please, I love you. May I have
an extra roll please, I love you." Once my father asked
me why I did this and I said, "Because I want it to be the
last thing you hear before you die." He wouldn't talk to
me for days after that. This is how I knew I'd given him
the wrong answer.

The right answer was, "Because I love you so much."

◦◦◦

In bed with my husband, I have to be gentle and slip free
so I won't wake him. I roll onto my back, pull the blankets
up, and stare at the ceiling until the tears stop. I lean my
head right, then left to get the water out of my ears.

◦◦◦

"What did you want to happen?" my husband asks.

I want this woman, this stranger, this mother to love
me.

I can't say it, though it's true.

I want her to worry for me.

I want her to be sorry.

I want her to make up for the mother I lost.

∽⊰⊱∾

At Target, I keep Phelan in her stroller and try to get Locklin to stick with me. I make him keep one hand on the stroller at all times, like something I picked up from a cop show. I used to think parents who put their kids on leashes were crazy or cruel, but now I'm not sure. Exhaustion and fear make a lot of things reasonable.

"Are you paranoid?" Blonde4Eva wanted to know. "We get that from mommy."

I don't know the line between paranoia and worry.

What I know are lists—to do, to remember, what to let go of, what to buy.

When I try to explain motherhood to friends like Sam who don't have children, I tell them sometimes my brain feels like a radio stuck between stations, a TV with the cable blown out. When I talk about motherhood with people who have children, we just make the sound of static, our shared password.

There are two kinds of people. People with kids and people without kids. The poet Gerry Locklin said that. Gerry Locklin has kids, a lot of them. My son was named for Gerry Locklin, a good and kind man who knows some things about the world.

When I talk about my kids to people who don't have children, those people talk about their own childhoods.

55

"I was just like that!" they say. They talk about their cats.

Our cart rolls through Target. I bend down and tuck Phelan's blanket so it doesn't drag. Locklin points with his one free hand. "Toys," he says, and I point at the list balanced on top of the stroller canopy. "Errands," I say, "then you can look."

It's easy to get distracted. Target confuses me the way Vegas casinos confuse me. There's something about the lights. In Vegas, I go into casinos at night and come out into morning. In Target, I go in with a list that says batteries, socks, diapers and come out with a bookshelf, a lava lamp, and a box of giant Pixie Stix.

Remember what you're here for, I tell myself, and check the list again.

✃

Not that it was beautiful, but that I found some order there. Anne Sexton said that.

When hypnotized, Anne Sexton used to say her name was Elisabeth. In the mental ward, Anne Sexton liked to imitate the symptoms of other patients until even her doctors were confused. "Highly suggestible," doctors said to explain Sexton's ideas about herself.

The day she committed suicide and left her own daughters motherless, Anne Sexton put on her dead mother's coat. She poured half a glass of vodka. She took off her wedding ring.

✃

There's you and me and there are other people. Another poet, Bei Dao, said that.

What I'm trying to remember: there are other people.

What I know: it can be a good thing to name yourself.

⤋

"Family," Blonde4Eva had called me, but to her it means something different.

Family is my son, my daughter, my husband, the ring I never take off, the ring we paid for with savings bonds and bought at a high-rise pawn shop in Pittsburgh and asked to be fitted with diamonds the size of coarse salt bits to make it shine a little. It's the ring I corkscrew on my finger when I'm nervous or scared or when I've forgotten something important.

⤋

Years later, Phelan and I will be back in Target and I will be apologizing because Phelan keeps yelling "I love you!" at a stranger in the bath aisle.

This future happens in February. Phelan is four. It's snowing. The snow caught in my daughter's hair makes her blonde pigtails curl. She's bundled in her pink down jacket, and one fluffed-up arm dangles over the cart. Her legs are strong and good, no more brace, and she happy-kicks them as I roll her through the store. She waves like a beauty queen.

"I love you!" Phelan yells again and again, and the

woman looks up from the bathmats she's holding, two slices of lime green shag.

I half-smile and say, "Sorry."

Earlier, Phelan and I stopped in the card section, a Valentine's Day display. Phelan loves the musical cards. She thinks they're magic and has to open every one. Today her favorite was a card that looked like a half-eaten box of chocolates. She plucked it from the rack, opened it.

"I love you!" it yelled.

Phelan laughed, squealed. She closed the card. She opened it. "I love you!" it yelled. She held the card over her head and waved it. She brought it back down and kissed it. She shook it, like she was waiting for something, fairies maybe, to fall out. She closed the card and opened it again and this time, she yelled back, "I love you!"

The rest of our shopping trip went like that. "I love you!" she yelled to the security guard checking receipts, to a sad couple with a basket of air fresheners, to a flop-haired kid in Digital Cameras. "I love you!" she yelled to the woman making popcorn at the concession stand, to the red-vested manager price-checking tennis shoes.

And now, "I love you!" Phelan says to this woman in a brown tweed coat, her arms laden with bathmats.

Everyone else had been at a distance, but this woman is close. I'm afraid Phelan might reach out and try to touch her. The woman stares as we push past. She doesn't smile or laugh. She seems horrified that I've let my daughter act out, and maybe she's right. Maybe I should have stopped this. I push Phelan faster and we turn into the next aisle. Plastic shower curtains covered with superheroes and angelfish. Toothbrush holders shaped like cities. All around us, there are so many towels. I reach into my pocket for my list and can't find it.

All these years of the same thing—lists full of batteries, socks, toothpaste. Years wheeling into this same store, where I've watched my children and myself grow older in grainy black-and-white pictures on the security cameras, our faces upturned, our hands waving like famous somebodies on TV.

My daughter saying I love you to all these strangers was cute.

Now it's become something else.

I scan her face for a sign of disappointment, regret, but those are my feelings, not hers.

"Be grateful for what you have," that old practiced advice, my own much-hated cliché.

Still, I am grateful. I exist. I am grateful for my family. I am grateful for my daughter, all smiling, pink-cheeked. She likes the angelfish curtains. She likes a soap dish shaped like a duck. I am grateful for the security cameras, the way they keep records.

We were here, are here. The cameras prove it.

Anne Sexton said, "At first it was private and then it was more than myself."

My daughter, her huge heart, the way she loves the world, is more than myself.

I'm overcome by the towels, all those soft blues, until I hear what I hoped would happen. The woman, one aisle over now, doesn't quite yell, but she says it loud enough.

"Love you, too," she says.

How a stranger feels shouldn't matter to me, but it does.

How my daughter feels should matter to me, and it does.

Phelan, distracted by the buzzing overhead lights, her own way of seeing, her singular beautiful life, doesn't notice.

9

A week after the Catholic Charities call, my husband and I decide to visit his parents in Michigan. It's a long drive, almost five hours. It takes a day to pack—diapers, juice boxes, bottles, changes of clothes, snacks, toys, stroller, bibs, collapsible high chair, safety gates. I remember to bring plastic bags for when Locklin throws up in the car. I keep the bags in a plastic milk jug with the side cut out. The milk jug is a craft I learned in Girl Scouts for the Recycling badge. "Re-imagining," our troop leader called it.

Locklin throws up a lot. He throws up when he's sick. He throws up when he's tired. He throws up from motion sickness and from boredom and whenever things haven't gone his way. For the past few years, everything I have smells like curdled milk and vomit.

On the way to day care, Locklin throws up because he doesn't want to go. He always throws up in exactly the same spot, right under a train trestle about one mile from the day care center. It took me a while to figure this out. Now I pack a change of clothes and change him in the back of the car. Then I go to work, teach my classes, knowing how I must look, how I must smell. I feel guilty about all of it.

"Some kids are gifted like that," the pediatrician says about Locklin's constant puking. We've come in for his annual check-up. It's also a pre-trip check, to make sure Locklin's o.k. to travel, that there's not something else going on.

The pediatrician wears ties with cartoons on them. His hair stands up in spikes and his eyes are big and round. He looks like a boy-man. He looks like a character from one of his ties. I can see why kids love him, but I've always felt uncomfortable around doctors, and this one is so nice and perky that his questions seem veiled, an interrogation.

"Is Mommy a good cook?" he asks my son.

"Are you a good sleeper?"

"Do you like TV? Or do you like sports better?"

"Which do you like best—carrots or apples?"

I feel myself grow small in the orange plastic chair while my son shifts back and forth on the exam table, the paper tearing under his bare legs. All around us, cartoon animals peer out from the wallpaper—rainbow-colored snakes and zebras, lions and giraffes all hidden in the design like a seek-and-find game, something to pass the time.

We've been coming to this doctor since my son was born. We've waited in this room a lot. I know where every zebra is hiding. I can point out the lions without looking.

I think the doctor can see me like that, too, his big anime eyes taking everything in.

I am a bad mother.

My son does not eat vegetables. He does not eat fruit unless juice boxes count. He fights bed time. He loves TV and doesn't get outside enough and he thinks sports are things kids are forced to do to entertain their parents.

My son is a gifted puker.

I feel all of this come down, a fault line. If I didn't work so much, if I kept him on a better schedule, if Mommy were a better cook, if I could pay more attention, if I were selfless, if.

"He looks good," the doctor says, and pats my son's leg, then my leg. He hands me paperwork and a list of parenting guidelines, safety tips, inoculation schedules.

My mother, the mother who raised me, was a nurse. She hated doctors—probably a byproduct of her job— but she was afraid of them, too. She used to change the bandages on my leg casts before we'd go for an appointment. She'd bring home supplies from the hospital where she worked. She used to scrub me and re-bandage the casts, then coat them in white shoe polish so they shined. She'd dress me like we were going to church. She'd dress herself to match. We'd smell blameless, Ivory soap and baby powder.

"Doctors," my mother would say, and click her tongue against her teeth. "They think their shit doesn't stink."

In the papers Catholic Charities sent me, there are medical reports and reports from social workers, accounts of their house visits after my adoption. My mother, I knew, worried she'd be seen as a bad mother, though there was another fear. She could be labeled unfit. I could be taken away. I could be sent back. "The client has articulated a persistent fear of this," one social worker reported about my mother, "though there is no indication that such fear is warranted. The baby is doing well and seems happy. She appears well cared for and loved."

"Thank you," I say to the pediatrician as he hands me the list of guidelines. I read it over and make mental checks. Use a car seat. Childproof outlets. Be careful around stairs.

"You don't know how much I worry," my mother used to say as she wrapped the wet plaster gauze around and around my legs.

I had no idea what she meant until I did.

❦

One time I saw my son's pediatrician at the mall. He looked smaller there. He was chasing his own kids, one boy and one girl, around the mall's padded play area. His kids had crawled into the trunk of a play tree and refused to get out.

"Come on now," he said. "Time to go."

His kids wedged themselves tighter into the tree as he began counting backwards from ten. In the mall's fluorescent light, his shoes seemed less shiny, his pants cheaper, wrinkled. His hair had gone flat. His cartoon smile looked forced and he seemed tired.

This made me like him more.

IO

༃

On the way to Michigan, the kids watch videos. They like *Thomas the Tank Engine*. Thomas is a whiny blue train with a big number 1 on his side. He and his bloat-faced train friends live on the Island of Sodor. They're afraid of many things—ghosts, lightning, the dark. They are always proper and cloying and very British.

"Well bust my buffers," Thomas says when he's upset, then he apologizes.

Thomas was created by a Reverend and his son, which means there are a lot of one-dimensional lessons. Thomas is the littlest train, so he's the hero. There's Gordon, a blustering express, all puff and hubris. And there are the evil Diesels, with their black smoke and dastardly eyebrows. All trains report to a station master, Sir Topham Hatt. Sir Topham Hatt is fat. He looks like Andrew Carnegie. He looks like Mussolini. His goal, like Mussolini's, is to see his trains run on time.

Sir Topham Hatt is often voiced by George Carlin. George Carlin used to do a skit—"Seven Dirty Words You Can't Say on Television." His book, *When Will Jesus Bring the Pork Chops?*, was banned at Wal-Mart.

Parenting demands the death of irony.

Parenting requires suspension of disbelief.

"If I have to watch that fucking Thomas movie one more time, I'm going to stab myself," my husband says, but he watches it over and over. He plays with the toys, one in each hand, drives miles to buy collector's items, and does voices to make our kids laugh.

Parenting demands this and other things, too.

⇜⫯⫯⇝

A few months back, my husband took Locklin out in a huge storm to buy a new Thomas toy. Locklin collects these wooden trains and train tracks and accoutrements expensive enough to be sold in designer boutiques. The weather had been o.k. when they left, but it kicked up fast. The storm took down trees and power lines. There were flash floods. A tornado watch blared on the Emergency Broadcast System, a series of wails I could feel in my teeth.

I was in tears by the time my son and husband came dripping through the door.

"I thought something awful happened to you," I said.

They looked at me like I was the kind of woman who could feel an Emergency Broadcast in her teeth.

"Like what?" my son said, and shrugged.

⇜⫯⫯⇝

My father would make me promise. "Don't let anything ever happen to you," and I would promise, even though

66

what he asked was impossible. I knew even when I was
very young that my father did not get close to many people. He was afraid of losing anyone he loved. When he
adopted me and became a parent, it made him feel more
secure and more vulnerable all at once. I understand this
now the way I understand my mother's worries, her own
fear of loss.

When people talk about adoption, they talk about
what matters more—nature or nurture. There is so much
of my parents in me I barely believe in blood.

ᴇᴏ{}ᴏᴣ

The night of the storm, I held my son and pressed my
face against his wet hair until he worked himself free. He
stepped back two paces, out of reach.

"Look. Cool, right?" he said, and held up his new toy,
a mountain tunnel with a boulder at the top.

The boulder was set with a trick trigger. It could roll
off any time a train passed through the tunnel. The sur-
prise, the not-knowing, was supposed to be fun.

Outside, the storm raged on, but my husband and
son were home safe. Locklin flicked the trigger to show
how the boulder tumbled down the mountain. He added
it to the tracks set up in the living room. He ran a train
through the tunnel again and again. Sometimes the boulder stayed put and the train made it through. Sometimes
it didn't.

The boulder could crush a train in its tracks, or not.

11

I chase Locklin around my in-laws' house. I try to keep him from hurting himself. I try to keep him from breaking things. The house is beautiful—lots of hard wood and glass. There are gold-edged collectible plates on the walls. The plates have inspirational sayings on them, Bible verses. The plates are decorated with seagulls, lighthouses, girls in straw hats. There is a china cabinet. There are stairs.

"I only ever wanted to be a mother," my mother-in-law says. She is beautiful, like her house. Her blonde hair is styled. Her eyebrows are tattooed on. Her nails are pink seashells. She says, "I was perfectly content to be home with my children," and her voice is soft, still tinged with the roll of the West Virginia hills where she grew up.

My mother-in-law keeps a stack of bibles and prayer guides on the living room end table. One of the guides is pink and flecked with bluejays. *A Woman's Guide to The Word*. My mother-in-law has a lot of ideas about what women and mothers should be. I'm sure I don't fit any of them, but she's too kind and polite to say so.

My parents-in-law are born-again Christians. My husband and I are not. I am Catholic—not the old-world Irish Catholic horror I was born into, but the American Catholic I was raised in and thought bad enough. I'm pretty sure born-again Christians think Catholics are heathens. They have good reason. Catholics have nuns we call Sisters and priests we call Fathers and lifelike renderings of Jesus on the cross, right down to his lips and abs and eyebrows. And there is always alcohol, the blood of Christ as interpreted by Riunite. There's gambling, too—Keno, Roulette, Lucky 7s.

"Seven is God's number," Father Ackerman, the priest at St. Regis explained to me once at a church-carnival card game. Father Ackerman turned his eyes to heaven, as if the god of 7s would bless and keep him and let him hit it big with the pair of twos he was holding. When he smiled, Father Ackerman showed his teeth, yellow, ground down like he'd been gnawing on bones. His gums and lips were stained purple from wine. His earlobes were fat and hairy as gerbils. "The devil's in the 6s," he said, then leaned in. "Never trust a 6."

I was born on the sixth of February.

Father Ackerman didn't like me.

❧

I won ten dollars and an Ouija board at a St. Regis bingo when I was 12. I still can't explain the Ouija board, the Catholic Church being the center for exorcisms. I can't explain it any more than I can explain why, during the

70

sleepovers and play-seances of my childhood, the board seemed to work. The pointer glided over letters and spelled out garbled messages from the other side. My friends and I asked the usual questions—the names of boys we'd marry, how many children we'd have, if we'd be rich, famous, how old we'd be when we died.

If we asked something the board didn't like, that question about death for instance, the pointer would slide over the word "goodbye" and all of us would groan and pinkie-swear we didn't make it move. We were young girls, our bodies pipe-cleaners and glitter-glue, google eyes and paste. We were raised on the *Wonderful World of Disney*. We wanted to believe in magic. We'd clap our hands for Tinker Bell. We'd kiss the feet of statues and drink holy water and speak in tongues if we thought it would make us special and beautiful and loved very much.

None of us wanted to ruin anything, not really.

⁓⊙⊰⊱⊙⁓

These days I'm mostly ambivalent about church. I think it would be nice to be the kind of person who could believe in such things, to see good and evil as polarities, to understand this world and the next as sturdy boxes to store souls in.

"It's a leap of faith," my father-in-law, who grew up in the Bronx and spent years in the merchant Marines, says. He is a good man who knows the truth about the world but chooses to believe in people anyway.

"Plus it'd be easier to control the kids if you took them

to church," my father-in-law says as Locklin runs loops and looks like he might puke on his grandfather's shoes.

"Who is Church?" my son says when anyone brings it up, like Church is the name of a wacky neighbor he doesn't want to visit.

"Jesus loves cookies," my daughter will say later, and she'll mean Christmas.

≈§≈

My husband, having grown up with too much church, despises it. When he was very young, it terrified him. The church his parents took him to showed movies of snake handlers. People convulsed when they felt the spirit move. For years, my husband was afraid his mother would be taken away on Judgment Day, and that he, a sinner who didn't like leaving bible tracts in the pockets of clothes for sale at Walmart, would be left behind. He imagined his mother would be lifted through the clouds like a toy in a crane game, and he'd be stuck on the ground, a motherless, unloved child, his own orphan fantasy.

"I'll just hold onto your ankles," he'd tell her, and she'd explain he couldn't do that. When he asked who she loved more, him or God, she said, "God."

≈§≈

"I only ever wanted to be a mother," my mother-in-law says.

She is a placid lake and I am the whirlpool, running after my son, both of us in socks, both of us trying not to slip and knock over one of the glass angels scattered on shelves around the house. Phelan, her legs spread by the hard plastic brace, bounces on my hip, a cowgirl in a saddle.

"You look like a crack whore," my husband will joke later when he sees the bruise.

12

Phelan and I sleep in one bedroom. Locklin and my husband sleep in another. I'm wedged into the bend of a futon. The futon frame is in my spine. Phelan is sleeping in her portable crib. She has to sleep in her leg brace, hips socketed and healing, which means she's stuck in one spot on her back like a paperweight.

The brace makes me sad, but it doesn't seem to bother Phelan much. "Temporary," the doctor said, and it will be true. Within a year, she'll be fine. "She's not like you," the doctor said.

Right now, though, braced or not, my daughter is a good sleeper, so peaceful. Still I try not to move around too much because I don't want to wake her.

In the next room, my husband is sprawled with our son on the double bed. I can hear them both snoring. Their snores sound wet. I'm sure they're both drooling. I imagine the puddles growing on the pillows, little Rorschach sketches under their lips.

My husband drove the whole way here. I was on puke-and-movie duty. I switched the videos. I kept a plastic bag ready in case Locklin got sick, which he did, but only once.

"Not bad, right?" Locklin said as I ran a cool wash-cloth over his mouth, and I said, "Much better."

My husband's exhausted, too, but I'm viciously jealous of sleep—anyone's, but especially his. No matter what my husband does with our children, and he does a lot, I believe I do more, even if it's not fair, even if it's not true. I believe there is some kind of distance between my husband and our children, a distance that doesn't exist for me.

Some days it feels as if my children never left my body. I imagine our DNA, three dancing fountains merged into one. I imagine our actual bodies fused, tendriled arms and legs braided like bread.

≈⊰⊱≈

"Bread is serious business," my mother said when she tried to teach me a family recipe for paska, Easter bread, the sweet braided loaves I loved as long as I could remember and wanted as an adult to make my own.

"Bread is nothing to mess around with," my mother said and slapped my hands to show me how to knead deep, the muscles in her arms urgent as an ambulance.

Where we were headed, I didn't know.

"It's time you learned," she said, and I said, "I'm trying."

She said, "When I'm dead, then what?"

≈⊰⊱≈

At 3 a.m., my cell phone rings. It's out of reach, so I have to climb out of the futon to get it. The futon creaks and sounds like a tree falling, but Phelan sleeps through it. I grab the phone and go next door into the bathroom. The light is fluorescent and pink and my eyes take a while to focus. I don't recognize the number, so I don't pick up, and wait for the voicemail message instead.

"You bitch," the voice says.

I don't recognize it, have never heard it before, but I know it's my sister, Blonde4Eva. I don't remember giving her my phone number but I must have.

"You fucking bitch," she says again. Her voice is thick. The word "bitch" has three syllables. She's drunk, at least that.

I can't remember the last time anyone has called me a bitch and meant it.

I can't remember ever hearing so much hate in a voice, especially from someone who, our birth stories aside, is a stranger.

You bitch, she says, the words like fists against the phone.

Blonde4Eva says I've ruined everything.

She says she needed us all to be together and now look.

She says she hopes I'm happy.

She says, "Mommy's furious."

She says, "No one knew." She says, "You were my secret."

My mind turns cruel. I imagine her, cross-eyed, slump-breasted, poodle-permed. I twist her image into something cartoonish until there's enough distance between us, until I'm sure she looks nothing like me, is nothing like me, until I know we could sit next to each other on the bus and never notice we shared a mother.

Cruelty is a bandage—mine, hers. I understand this and it doesn't change anything.

She's smoking. I can hear the pull of the cigarette, the exhale of the smoke, the crack and burn. She says everyone is mad at her when it's me they should be mad at.

"Call me back," she says, and it's almost childlike, the words pulled like taffy into a question. But she's the one who calls back, again and again until I shut the phone off. I feel sick, like I might throw up, but I don't. I think it might be good to be gifted like my son. I think if I could just convince my body to throw up, I might stop shaking.

In the morning, there are twelve voicemails, each one angrier and less coherent than the one before.

13

I don't know what to do with the messages. They're awful. I can't listen to them, but erasing them would be like erasing evidence. The voice with its smoke-choked Pittsburgh accent, the way the words stretch and strain, like a garbage bag filled to bursting.

You.

Bitch.

"Who is she to talk to me like that?" I say to my husband.

I'm standing in my in-laws' kitchen. The light is bright, golden. The décor is pears. They are stenciled everywhere. There are pears on the dishes, pears on the mugs, stained-glass pears on the windowpanes. Odysseus had a taste for pears. Pears from enchanted gardens helped with his nausea, his homesickness. Pears helped him forget.

"You cannot truly know or love *The Odyssey* until you've read it in the original Greek," Professor Hinman said in grad school. Professor Hinman had a collection of hand puppets he'd use when he taught *The Odyssey*. "To help us translate," he said. Odysseus was buff and bearded, homeless and lost. The Cyclops, in his bowl cut and fur, looked like Ringo Starr. The Sirens were two blondes sewn together on one puppet mitt. The Sirens were twins, except for their mouths—one heart-lipped and loving, one vicious and fanged.

To my husband, I say again, "Just who the hell does she think she is to say that to me?"

I'm holding a knife. I'm trying to slice a bagel in two. I'm not thinking about the knife. I hold the bagel in my palm and saw the blade into my skin.

"Cut away from yourself," my mother always said.

I put my palm to my mouth and suck. It tastes like salt and metal and sesame from the bagel I was working on. I pull my palm back and inspect the ragged cut right between the heart and life lines. It's not deep, but still. The blood is coming up in spots, flecks. There is a sting, more like a papercut. I throw the knife into the sink.

"Fuck this," I say, and I'm grateful my in-laws are at church.

"Who's church?" Locklin would say, confused.

Dr. Hinman wanted his students not to be confused. "Sometimes it's easier just to visualize how the words play out," he'd say, and dance Odysseus across a desk.

I don't know how Blonde4Eva's words play out. I'm confused and I'm furious. Anger comes after grief and fear, a logical thing, but I can't sort this. I want the truth and I want the lie I was born with. I want connection and I want to get as far away as possible.

Look—here's the knife in the sink. Here are Odysseus' heart-sick pears on the dish towel my husband has snagged off the fridge to sop up my blood.

My husband lays the dish towel on the counter. He holds my wrist, turns my palm up, inspects the damage.

"I think it's stopped bleeding," he says, then as a joke adds, "you bitch."

It will be a long time before any of this is funny.

⊰⊱

After church, over bagels I did not bleed on, my husband tells his parents about the calls. He tells them about my search, everything that's happened. I focus on spreading cream cheese on my bagel, all the way to the edges. I make circles with the plastic knife as if it's very important intricate work, the circles connecting to other circles to other circles, a universe expanding, a mandala to bite and swallow, to create and destroy, forever and ever, amen.

My mother-in-law says, "That's terrible."

My father-in-law says, "What would possess someone to do that?"

I don't want to talk about it, but I do.

It would be impolite not to, I think.

"Imagine," my mother-in-law says again, her face an open window trying to let air in.

"It's o.k.," I say, and try to sound like it is.

I want to make up for sleeping late, for not going to church. I want to be seen as a good person. Forgiving. The kind of person who could shrug off a birth mother's rejection, a birth sister's insistence that I am, without doubt, a bitch.

I add more cream cheese to my bagel and swirl. I

take a bite. My hand stings. I open and close it to feel how much.

"People do what they can," I say.

Like my mother, the mother who raised me, I speak in clichés when things get bad.

"Never use a word or phrase you're accustomed to hearing or seeing in print," I tell my students, something I stole from George Orwell.

It's a great rule for writing.

It's not always useful for living.

14

Years ago, I saw a palm reader in a basement storefront in New York. She held my wrists, turned my palms up, both hands. "This," she said, tracing a finger down the lines of my left hand, "is what you were born with." Then she traced a finger on my right palm. "And this," she said, "is the map you make yourself."

Then she asked for $50. She took Mastercard and Visa, not Discover.

◦◦|◦◦

On my left hand, the life line is thin, shallow, forked. The heart line is severed. It stops, breaks, then picks back up a notch down, a detour. On my right hand, the lines are deeper, braided, almost red. Where the lines are broken on the left, they've seemed to heal and scar over into long helixes on the right.

I've always liked to think this means something.
I've always wanted to believe in the order of things.

◦◦|◦◦

When I ask about my sister, "Who does she think she is?" I don't ask, "Who do I think I am?" I feel guilt and shame, as if my sister's words are my words, her anger and need my anger and need, as if I can't take anything back. You bitch, I tell myself.

"What kind of person doesn't give a medical history?" I'd asked about my birth mother.

What kind of person goes on opening boxes that demand to stay shut?

⁓⟨⟩⁓

"She screamed and screamed at me," the Catholic Charities counselor said about my birth mother. "Imagine."

I've found my roots, the map of what I was born with.

15

Before I started my own search, I read Linda Carroll's memoir, *Her Mother's Daughter*.

Linda Carroll is the mother of Courtney Love, spokesperson for everything that money and drugs and fake boobs and Versace can't fix. The book isn't a tell-all, though Courtney hasn't spoken to her mother in years. It's mostly about Carroll, who was adopted, trying to find her way as a mother while trying to understand her own history. It's about Carroll's search for her birth mother, who turned out to be the writer Paula Fox, whose own book about giving up her daughter for adoption, *Borrowed Finery*, I also read and loved.

"When I was growing up, people asked me how I felt about being adopted," Carroll writes. "I always said, 'It's not an issue.' I believed my own lie."

It was like a line lifted from my own childhood.

"It's not an issue," I'd say. When people pressed for more, I'd add, "My parents chose me." I'd make my voice a knife to slice the person asking the questions. I'd make my voice say, "You, you're the mistake, you're unwanted, not me."

Always cut away from the self.

After Carroll sought out and found Fox, whose literary passion was so much like her own, she says she felt her life made more sense.

"She's like me," Carroll told the *San Francisco Chronicle*. "Kids need a certain kind of mirroring when they're growing up, and my adoptive parents didn't know how to mirror me because I was so different from them. But with Paula, I saw so much of myself, so much of my own history in her story."

My mother and I were not each other's mirrors, even when she dressed us in matching outfits she'd sewn herself, even when she delighted at the bank teller who would say, "She looks just like you. She has your eyes," and the flirty bank manager with the Grecian Formula comb-over, too-short pants and white socks would add, "Are you two twins?"

Growing up, I hid in my room. I liked to lie under my bed and stare up at the box springs and terrify myself by imagining spiders in the coils. I wrote poems and copied dialogue from *Dennis the Menace* comic strips. I re-arranged my mother's spice cabinets and lined up the spices according to color, the way my mother arranged her shoes. I didn't have much need for company, other than books and my Kansas albums and my dog. I liked to sleep in my closet, a dark, dank, closed-in space that, when I think of it now, seems like a womb.

"Why can't you be normal?" my mother would say.

❦

"Not blood of my blood nor flesh of my flesh, but heart of my heart," my mother would write on heart-shaped notes she'd tuck in my lunchbox. She'd recite the lines to me at bedtime and, later, when she was very sick, she'd repeat them as a mantra before she went into surgery and was afraid she would die.

At the very end, she shortened it and said only, "Heart."

I said it back.

I'm not sure where she first learned the phrase, which was lifted from a cheesy 1950s poem, "The Answer (to an adopted child)," by Fleur Conkling Heyliger. The poem first ran in the *Saturday Evening Post*. My mother did not read *The Saturday Evening Post*, though she liked Norman Rockwell's cover paintings. "Wholesome," she said about the Rockwell posters hanging in her doctor's office.

My mother read *Reader's Digest* and *TV Guide*. She read "Dear Abby" columns.

"That Abby tells you what's what," my mother used to say.

When Abby coughed up a bit of useful advice, my mother would clip the column and stick it on the fridge. She'd point to it and say, "Now that's real beer."

After my mother died, I left her voice on her answering machine for a long time. I left the light on in her living room so when I drove by, I could convince myself she was in there, up late, reading. I left her crochet needles in the coffee-table drawer and still have the scrap of blanket she was working on. I left her tweezers in their place in the soap dish and her robe where she'd left it the last time she'd worn it, draped over the back of a kitchen chair.

I listened to her answering machine message over and over. I left it like that until my Aunt Velma told me it was frightening people.

Just before this, Aunt Velma, a Jehovah's Witness, had come into my mother's house and taken all the drugs my mother had stockpiled in shoeboxes for years. Painkillers, codeine, heart pills, blood pressure pills, sleeping pills. Some of the pills dated back decades and were useless except as a catalogue of my mother's suffering. Aunt Velma had a key to the house. She let herself in. She loaded up the trunk of her rusted Toyota, then drove to The Kingdom Hall and doled drugs to her fellow Witnesses, who she said didn't believe in doctors.

"And I don't believe in waste," she said. "My sister didn't either. Unlike some people."

After my mother died, Aunt Velma did not refer to her as my mother. My mother became her sister. Aunt Velma became simply Velma. I became some people.

"It's like that with some families," the Catholic Charities counselor explained.

"You didn't grow under my heart," the last line of Heyliger's poem reads, "but in it."

"It's creepy," my aunt said, about the answering machine.

About the drugs, she said, "We got the good stuff."

When I erased the answering machine message, I erased the only recording I had of my mother's voice. With Blonde4eva's messages, it doesn't take nearly as long. I listen to them once more, shaking, then press delete.

I think this finishes things.

"What's done is done," my mother would have said. "Let sleeping dogs die." Sometimes she mixed her metaphors and got her clichés wrong. "You get more bees with honey than you do with vinegar," she'd say, when she wanted me to be nice.

"You mean flies," I'd say. "Bees make their own honey."

"You think you know everything," she'd say, and bang the silverware into the drawer. "I could write a book about what you don't know."

⋘⟨⟩⋙

"And what was it you wanted to know?" the Catholic Charities counselor asked.

A medical history, I'd said.

But I wanted to know something that looked and moved and laughed and loved and was sad like me.

If Blonde4eva is what I look like, I want to cover her with a blanket, in mourning for everything that's lost and should stay lost.

89

16

My daughter's first word is *abre,* open. She learned it from *Dora the Explorer* (TV Show). This is my daughter. Kind, happy, trusting, *abre.* When I tuck her in at night, Phelan lies on her back and laughs. She kicks and swats the blankets off. She flings her arms open for a hug but more, as if she wants to take in everything, as if the whole world is the squishy blue ball it's made out to be in cartoons.

My son's first word was *duck.* When we'd drive under bridges, Locklin would shout from his car seat, "Duck!" and my husband and I would crouch and cower and pretend we were this close to having our heads sheared off. Locklin would nod, serious as concrete, like he already knew everything there was to know about danger and loss, like it was his job to keep us safe.

Abre. Duck.

I haven't thought of these as blood things before and now I do.

⁓⊰⊱⁓

It's almost Christmas, so the kids and I go to the Pittsburgh Mills Mall to visit Santa. Before we leave, Locklin snags last year's Santa picture from its spot on the fridge. I don't ask why.

"Don't wrinkle that," I say, my voice fast and sharp as a slap.

On the twenty-five minute drive, I feel guilty. It's been like that—my nerves, my temper, all these cliffs to jump. I want to scream and slap and go on slapping over small things, a Santa picture for Christ's sake, even though I swore I would never hit my children and I do not hit my children.

When she was dying, my mother said, "I'm sorry I wasn't a better mother. I'm sorry I was nervous all the time." She meant, I think, she was sorry for how she was when I was growing up. She had a kitchen drawer full of wooden spoons, different sizes and weights, and was a quick draw. When she couldn't get to the spoons fast enough, she used her hands to hit, which didn't hurt as much. Other times she'd take a pill and lock herself in her bedroom and wait for my father to get home. My father used a belt, a fancy one he never wore. The buckle was gold. It was large and heavy and had the initial G on it, though my father's name was Walt. "G for Gerald," my mother explained once, "his middle name," which didn't explain anything at all.

⋅⊷⧓⊶⋅

The Mills Mall is on the remote outskirts of Pittsburgh, in Frazer Township. Sometimes a bear wanders through the mall's automatic doors and state rangers set bear traps on the hillside near Sears. The Pennsylvania Gun Collectors host events at the mall's Expo Center. Last month, they held a Gun Bash and a Gun Bingo. All of this suits my mood.

"Duck!" Locklin yells, his almost-joke now, as we drive under the railroad trestles that dot the Pennsylvania Turnpike on our way here. I duck. "Safe!" Locklin yells like an umpire.

The calls from the woman who says she's my sister have stopped. Now I feel like I'm waiting, but I don't know for what. This is almost worse. My doctor's given me a prescription for Xanax. I break them in half at night to help me sleep. I try not to use them in the daytime. I use them in the daytime.

"Family history of mental illness?" the doctor asked, his head in a checklist, and I said, "I'm adopted." In the margins, he wrote "N/A."

Not applicable or not available? I wanted to say there's a difference.

⌖

Locklin is quiet on the drive to the mall. In the rearview mirror, I watch him examining the Santa picture. His eyes narrow. His tongue peeks from the corner of his mouth, the way it does when he's concentrating.

"Leave it," I say when he tries to take the picture into the mall, and he leaves it, face up, a red stain on the back seat.

93

We wait over an hour to see Santa. The line isn't long, but it takes time for Santa's helpers—two unhappy women in elf hats and Steelers jerseys—to help everyone decide on overpriced photo packages. I keep Phelan strapped in her stroller to stop her from ripping the heads off reindeer. Locklin examines fistfuls of fake, possibly toxic snow, like he's checking a crime scene.

Inside Santa's woodsy Wonderland, Santa and Mrs. Claus look like a miserable hillbilly couple holed up in a giant plastic tree. Mrs. Claus pretends to knit something, which gives her an excuse to ignore the children who clamber onto Santa's lap and try to whack his glasses off. Above Mrs. Claus' head, mechanical squirrels spasm over a pile of acorns. A pack of raccoons twitch their mangy tails. Bluebirds snap their beaks open and shut like claws. There isn't a candy cane in sight.

Still, when we get to the front of the line, Phelan squeals. She is all in pink—pink sweater set, pink tights. She looks like a fluff of cotton candy on Santa's knee.

She says her second word, the one that came weeks after *abre*.

She says, "Beautiful!"

"What's your name?" Santa says.

Phelan says, "Beautiful!"

Locklin, hands in pockets, explains things. "Her name's Phelan," he says. "My name's Locklin. Nice to meet you." He puts out his hand for Santa to shake, but Santa doesn't see it.

"Brelynn?" Santa says, cupping his ear.

"Phelan," Locklin says again.

"Kaylyn?" Santa says.

From the sidelines, I enunciate. "Fay Lynn. And his name is Locklin. Lock. Lin."

Before he can help it, Santa says, "What the hell kind of names are those?"

❧

Back in the minivan, Locklin holds up the Santa pictures, last year's and this new one, side by side.

He says, "You've got to be kidding me."

He says, "So you're saying that this guy," and he pauses. He thrusts last year's model forward. This Santa is younger, jollier, rosier. His nose is not gin-blossomed. He did not, as I remember, smell like cheese. "Is the same," he says, "as this guy?"

Locklin switches the pictures. Santa has aged three decades. His glasses, round wire-rims last year, are now square little bifocals that sit crooked on his nose. His teeth, chewing-gum-commercial white 12 months before, have gone yellow. His brown eyes are milky and blue as oysters. I look closer. I squint. I clear my throat.

"Well, sure," I say. My words are slow, careful, but my tone is off and my son knows it.

"You know, honey," I say. "Everybody gets older. Maybe Santa had a bad year. His job's very stressful."

Locklin just stares. He pushes the evidence closer to my face.

"Maybe Santa just needs sleep," I say, and laugh.

Locklin does not laugh. "It doesn't make sense," he says again. "It's just wrong."

95

I know what he means. I look into his eyes, the same color as mine, green Depression glass, and I see it: the confusion, the anger, the way it's hard to accept when the world and everything in it falls short.

The world promised my son a miracle.

It gave him a busted yo-yo instead.

"Santa's a liar," Locklin says.

Phelan, who doesn't know the word, starts to cry anyway.

17

When I was in graduate school, the poet Lucille Clifton came to read. She was dressed all in blue, her hair was a cloud. She looked like a kind nun or someone's benevolent aunt. She stood at the podium and seemed misplaced, puzzled, as if she'd been looking for her keys and ended up here in front of all these blank expectant faces. Then she tapped the podium's wooden sides gently, the way she might tap a cake to see if it was done.

"I spend a lot of time thinking about the names of things," she said. "Like, why is this a podium? Who decided that? Don't you wonder that too?"

We nodded our daisy heads.

Most of the faces were white, like mine.

Most of the people in that room had no idea what Lucille Clifton, a black woman who wrote about ancestry and loss and the importance of names, meant.

"No," she said. "Probably not."

꿱

My hair is blonde. My eyes are green. I'm tall, fat-nosed. I

97

have big hands, long fingers. The mother who raised me named me Lori. Lori: English origin, from the laurel tree, symbol of victory, honor, valor, hope. "People with this name have a deep desire for a stable loving family," the baby name book says.

"I just liked it," my mother said about my name.

≈⊙⟨⟩⊙≈

My birth mother named me Amelia. Amelia, from the German *amal*, meaning work, effort, strain. Famous Amelias: Amelia Bedelia, Minnie Driver, Amelia Earhart.

Amelia Earhart's childhood pet was a dog named James Ferocious. She once built a roller coaster in her backyard. She was infamous in her family for eating the last piece of candy and talking out of turn.

When Amelia Earhart got lost, she stayed lost.

Maybe some people in her life felt relieved about that.

18

🙕

I am 14 when my mother organizes a family photo shoot at the duck pond in Turtle Creek, a gift for my grandmother's 70th birthday. The duck pond is in the Catholic cemetery. It's pretty, a prime spot for wedding and family portraits, but the angle has to be right to keep tombstones out of the shots. At 14, I think this is funny.

The photographer, George—50-something, gaptoothed, tatty blazer—does not. George says, "Jiminy Christmas." George says, "Come on, people, work with me." George sucks air through his teeth when he's frustrated. Today he sucks a lot of air. Hands on hips, bent over, George looks like he's between steps in step aerobics. From behind, George looks like one of those cutouts sad housewives prop next to their garden gnomes. The cutouts look like mushrooms, but look closer and they're fat women bent over, all petticoats and butt cheeks.

"Now that's creative!" my mother said when she first saw one for mail order in the back of *Family Circle* magazine.

George looks like he'd rather do lingerie shots of sad housewives dressed as mushrooms than deal with this.

George says, "We'll get this sucker yet," like our family photo is something stubborn and painful, a splinter in his toe.

It might be the tombstones, it might be the lighting, but I'm deep into puberty and I loathe myself even more than I loathe George. I'm gawky, blonde, too tall. I'm wearing a cream-colored dress and everybody else is navy and gray. There's a mole the size of a pencil eraser on my cheek and the tingle of a new zit in my eyebrow.

Everyone else here looks the same—symmetrical, olive-toned, second-generation Italian immigrant shrubs.

Which of these things is not what it seems—mushroom or fat lady?

Which of these things doesn't belong? Apple, apple, horse, apple.

"You," George says to me. "Let's try you over here."

George moves me to the back row, far right.

Everyone else fits.

Almost everyone.

"And you," he says to my cousin Geri. "Over here." George claps his hands and corrals Geri, a year older than me and just as self-conscious, to the back row, left. She shifts side to side, like she has to pee. "Better," George says, and squints into his camera, then makes his dying balloon sound.

In the final shot, Geri and I look like we've crashed some other family's photo session. We look like mismatched bookends holding up some other family's story.

George tells my mother, "It's a wonderful thing to preserve one's family for posterity."

George says, "I think the recipient will be delighted."
George says, "Will you be ordering keychains?"

⚬๑⎮๑⚬

Like me, my cousin Geri was adopted. Different orphanage, different lineage. When she sees me, she says, "Hey stranger." She says, "You and me, we're strangers around here," then adds "thank god."

Geri's bi-racial. She knows it, I know it, but the rest of the family pretends it's not true. When my aunt and uncle adopted her, the agency told them Geri was Italian, with maybe a little Greek thrown in. Italian and Greek in a family where men were prone to Italian Stallion tattoos was fine. A Caucasian/African American mix, not fine. Unacceptable. An abomination. It's a horrible truth, but this was 1960s working-class Pittsburgh, and the money was in healthy white babies. The social workers at the agency knew this and Geri was such a sweet thing, never cried, never fussed.

"Highly adoptable," was the phrase social workers used.

I read that somewhere.

I was not highly adoptable. I was born crippled, two clubbed feet, and needed many surgeries. The only reason my parents ended up with me is because they were too old to qualify for a healthy white baby girl.

"We loved you from the moment we saw you," my father says and I believe him.

"We chose you," my mother says, and I know she has made herself believe she always had a choice.

My uncle, Geri's adopted dad, is a cop. My aunt cleans houses. They love Geri, too, but they grew up with segregation. They believed in segregation. They loved segregation. They still won't go into a swimming pool if black people are in there first. They call the fancy nuts they serve at Christmas nigger toes.

My aunt has tried for years to straighten my cousin's hair.

She tries to keep her daughter out of the sun.

She says, "What's wrong with you? Why do you get so dark?"

She says, "You look like you stuck your finger in a socket."

She says, "You get any darker, they'll ship you to Africa."

She says, "Do you want to be shipped to Africa?"

When our other cousins, two cruel boys who push our faces in the dirt and try to make us lick their feet, watch the Lakers on TV, they point to Magic Johnson, then to Geri.

They say, "Smile, Ger."

They size up Magic on the screen and say, "He looks just like you."

They say much worse than that.

But Geri is funny. She tells good jokes. She is often the brunt of her own jokes, so as orphans go, the family likes her better than me.

Years from now, when I go away to college, the aunts will say, "You can't hide forever. Someday you're going to have to get a real job." When I go to grad school, they will say, "What do you want to be? An educated bum?"

When Geri goes into the Army, the aunts will say how proud they are. They will show pictures of Geri playing basketball in Germany. They will show pictures of her lounging on a beach in Crete. In those pictures she'll be smiling. She'll be very beautiful and very dark. She'll be wearing shorts and tank tops the color of the Mediterranean. Her teeth will be white sand.

"I tell her," my aunt, her mother, will say. "She should stay out of the sun. People will get ideas. But look how happy she is. She's finally getting to see the world. My Geri baby."

When she becomes a cop like her father before her, the aunts will say what a good cop she'll be because she always has been so kind and good. She's been that way since the day she was picked up from that orphanage. Everyone will agree. Geri has been grateful from the start. She has always said thank you. She has always said please.

Those may have been my cousin's first words, to hear the aunts tell it over glasses of red wine and pasta. Geri always had a good temperament, they will say.

Then they'll look at me and sigh.

I am not a model orphan.

I am moody and outspoken. I lack gratitude, especially for a born cripple. I have been known to eat the last piece of candy in the box.

I feel guilty about this.

Guilt doesn't change anything.

❧

"Smile," George the photographer says, "Smile like you mean it, not like you're going to bite somebody."

I give George what feels like a real smile. I try to think of something happy. I think of a song I like by Boston. I go through the lyrics in my head. I get stuck on a line and forget about smiling.

"Teenagers," George says.

Everything about him is helium.

❧

It is no small thing to confess sins to Father Ackerman, with his nasty hairy ears and breath like a sweatsock. It is an easier and better punishment to be gnawed by squirrels. But the guilt gets to me, and every once in a while, when I've done something awful, I ask my mother to take me to confession.

"That Father Ackerman," my mother says. "He doesn't pussyfoot around."

Every Sunday, I endure Father Ackerman's long sermons about Jesus and the cripples. My mother elbows me to pay attention to the parts she is sure are meant especially for me.

"See what you learn if you listen instead of running your mouth all the time?" my father said after a mass where Father Ackerman encouraged parents to beat gratitude into children who seem immune to it. Father Ackerman suggested parents use their hands for beatings, so children would feel that physical connection.

"So," my father said. "Who wants doughnuts?"

Sometimes I feel God is talking right to me, through Father Ackerman, his creepy, hairless hands pressing down on my shoulders like cement weights. I'd come to my parents through Catholic Charities. My cousin had come to her parents through another branch of Catholic Charities. This God, Father Ackerman's God, must have had something to do with our adoption miracles. Still, when Father Ackerman waits at his farewell spot by the baptismal font after every mass, when he admonishes us to "Go with God," he sounds more like a mafia boss than any messenger of Christ.

"You never see the good in people," my mother says. "You never say anything nice," she says, and turns her mouth upside down.

I want to tell her I try, but maybe she's right. Still, Father Ackerman's church isn't much of a church. It's a school basement and the confessional booth is a repurposed janitor's closet. The kneeler creaks and is uneven, so sinners have to balance on it like a seesaw. The light outside, which is supposed to turn from green to red when you kneel down, doesn't always turn and people often walk in on each other mid-confession. It's like catching someone in the bathroom.

The confessional smells like old-lady powder and worms after rain. It smells like damp wood. It smells, I think, like a coffin once the undertaker closes the lid and locks a body in.

Father Ackerman sits behind the yellowed plastic privacy screen, that breath of his oozing through the pinholes. He cocks a hairy ear. I tell him I do not honor my father and mother. I tell him I am an ungrateful child.

He says, "Didn't your parents take you out of that orphanage?"

About my sins, he asks, "How many times?"

The Catholic Church is big on counting things. Sins need to be tallied so the proper number of Hail Marys and Our Fathers can be dished as penance. I don't tell Father Ackerman my sins are uncountable, an ongoing problem, something genetic and probably incurable.

"Ten," I say, a good number, a round number, perfect as Bo Derek in cornrows.

Father Ackerman gives me the prescription to make me blameless. He makes the sign of the cross, his wax-museum hand a shadow behind the screen.

He tells me all is forgiven.

He calls me his child.

He tells me to go and sin no more.

I balance my weight on the kneeler.

I try not to creak.

∞

We are having our usual Sunday dinner at my grand-mother's house when my aunts mention my cousin's good temperament one too many times.

I am the worst kind of teenager—a seether.

"You mean smart ass," my father says.

"It's in you to always look at the worst in things," my mother says.

"She's been that way from the moment you picked her up," my aunts say.

"You never can tell what you'll get," my grandmother says, like adoption is a grab-bag sale.

I sit and seethe. Then I cover my plate with my nap-kin. I push my chair from the table. I walk to my grand-mother's sewing machine. My grandmother keeps a huge stack of old *Pennysavers* piled on top of the machine, which hasn't worked for years. My grandmother is over 250 pounds and a keeper of things she does not use. My grandmother has a great passion for food—a minute ago she took a half-eaten pork chop from my plate, chewed it down to marrow, then sucked the marrow dry.

I think I love my grandmother, but I am angry.

I am almost always angry.

I pull a couple dusty *Pennysavers* from the pile, and open the Adoptable Pets sections.

Then I read the ads out loud.

Mixed breed. Cockapoo. Bull terrier named Butch, free to loving home.

The phrase "good temperament" shows up in nearly every one.

When I'm done, I fold the *Pennysavers* and put them

back onto my grandmother's about-to-topple pile. I look at my cousin, who looks past me at the crucifix above my head. The crucifix is a fire hazard. Jesus is lost in a jungle of desiccated palm fronds.

"We've had our shots, too," I say.

Everyone stops chewing. My mother points her fork like she might stab me. My Uncle Bus drinks his Budweiser from a can. He crushes the can, drops it into the pail next to him, and pops his standby. My Uncle Tony stares at the Steelers game on mute on the TV. The stereo my grandmother keeps on all day every Sunday keeps cranking out polkas, all that happy music, barrels of fun. The aunts click their tongues.

My grandmother says, "You will have manners in my house, young lady," then she digs into her ravioli before it gets cold.

Back home I'll be grounded, but it's worth the laugh Geri and I share out on my grandmother's side porch where we'll dangle from clothesline poles and consider whether or not we're housebroken, or if we've had all our shots, or how we could ever be good with children.

⋖⦿⦚⋗

Sometimes our mothers encourage us to find our birth mothers.

"Maybe she'd know what to make of you," my aunt says to Geri.

"Maybe it would help you feel more settled," my mother says to me.

I know my birth name. I know my birth mother's name. It would be easy enough.

"It would be good for you to find out," my mother says.

Other times, the idea frightens her. "Some rocks are better left alone," she says. "Let sleeping snakes lie."

"You mean dogs," I say.

"You probably get your smart mouth from *her*," my mother says, that one syllable whirring in her throat like a vacuum cleaner. "Someday you're going to choke on all those smart words of yours."

Then my mother goes and dusts something.

⊷⊶

My mother thinks scientists should come up with a way to match adoptive kids' personalities with the personalities of the families interested in adopting them. One day she tells me this. "That way they'd get a good match," she says. "Like things with like things. It would be better for everybody."

We've been fighting—chores, homework. There's always something between us.

My mother's face when she says this, though, is flat as a card deck. It isn't something she says out of anger. It's something she's been considering for a long time.

⊷⊶

"Matchmaker, matchmaker make me a match," George, the photographer at the cemetery, sang as he shuffled my cousin and me, trying to find a spot where we fit.

He didn't mean anything. He was the kind of guy who liked musicals. He was the kind of guy who probably had *Fiddler on the Roof* on tape.

⊷⊶

"I don't know where you came from," my mother says when she disapproves of something—my crushed-blue-velvet-button-fly-hip-hugger jeans or the expensive perfume with real pheromones I douse myself in. The perfume smells like shoe polish and the fake deer pee hunters in our neighborhood spritz to make themselves invisible to prey. The hip-huggers give me a terrible case of camel toe. I don't know any of this.

All I know is it's important to spend hours rolling my blonde bangs into two vertical sausages. All I know is I hate my mother.

It doesn't help that I'm clumsy and my mother likes things neat.

"You're a mistake waiting to happen," she says.

My mother, master of language.

⊷⊶

Mistakes are not blood things. Or maybe they are. It depends on what you watch on TV, *Oprah* or *Maury Povich*. It depends on which magazine cover you stop for at the grocery store.

One tells you you've made the life you own.

The other believes in paternity tests, a studio audience, body guards pillared at four corners of the stage.

"Tell the audience how you're feeling right now," Maury Povich always says, right after the big reveal. He pushes his microphone close and the camera moves in and there's a pause, a moment when there's just a mouth, open, slack, no words coming out, because really, what can anyone say at a moment like that?

∽⊶⟨⟩⊷∾

"Smile," George the photographer said, and Geri smiled big.

She wanted to please.

"Not every day's a funeral, you know," George said to me.

I tried.

I did.

I do.

∽⊶⟨⟩⊷∾

"I think it looks nice," my aunt said when she saw the family photo. She ran her thumb over the spot where Geri stood, like something was there, a spot, a speck. She rubbed at the image of her daughter, like she could blur it out and make it blend.

This is years before Photoshop, when people in pictures actually looked the way they looked in real life and there was nothing anyone could do about it.

∽⊶⟨⟩⊷∾

Looking back, if such things as genetic personality matching had been possible, neither I nor Geri would have ended up in our family.

"And that would have been a bad thing how?" Geri would want to know.

Both Geri and I are in our thirties when she finds her birth family. Geri's birth mother is white. Her dad's black. She has full brothers and sisters. It was a timing thing, they say about giving her up.

Geri says, "Now I know where I get my sense of humor."

She says, "It's good to know some things."

She says, "I look a lot like my dad."

At first things seem good, but then Geri cuts off contact with her birth family. She won't say why. My aunt, her mother, starts rumors, though.

The birth family asked for money. They asked for favors. Cops can do things. Those people wanted those things. That's what my aunt calls them. Those people. "You know how those people are," my aunt says.

When my aunt goes on blaming black people for destroying Braddock, when she says things like "those welfare jiggaboos let their babies run around without diapers and they piss on everything," my cousin will still visit her every other day. She will take her to the doctors and bring groceries and take her to church and stay during the service when her mother needs her to do that, even though Geri has never been much for church.

My cousin will never shut her mother out of her life. I don't know why.

⚜

"You're a good person," I tell Geri. We're talking about something else. She's been telling a story about the time she went to arrest a guy and was worried she hurt him because there was blood. She was upset until she realized the blood was hers. The guy had stabbed her in the thigh and she didn't feel it.

"Good? Hell no. I punched him in the head after that," she says.

"I mean your heart's good," I say, and she looks at me like I've said something ridiculous, like I've told her she has a good temperament. "I mean you're not like most cops," I say, "the way they get hard. The way they stop feeling things."

She nods, and I nod, but I don't mean cops really.

I mean people.

I mean me.

⚜

Once on the South Side of Pittsburgh, my friend Trish and I met two cops in a bar. We were talking, playing a trivia game. It was an electronic tabletop game. I was winning. The category was literature or maybe rock 'n' roll. Those are my favorites. I like bar trivia games. I like any game that lets me think a bit while I drink to keep myself from thinking too much.

113

One of the cops took my friend Trish out back to do some blow. The other cop sat with me at the bar, a little sad because I was less fun than Trish. I didn't want to sleep with him. I didn't want to do what he said were the very primo drugs he'd snagged in a traffic stop from a real dirt bag. A real dirt bag with very primo blow.

The cop had a bad mustache. It was a sad mustache, or maybe it was a disappointed mustache. Maybe the mustache was disappointed because I'd disappointed the cop and on better days the mustache may have looked better, perkier, more alive. Right then, though, it sat on the cop's lip like old lettuce. I stared at the mustache when I talked and felt bad about it.

I said, "My cousin's a cop."

He said, "Oh yeah. Which precinct?"

I told him.

He said, "Really? What's her name?"

I told him.

He said, "Oh yeah. I know her. Good cop. Good kid. She was a foster kid or adopted or some shit. She has problems with her family. Trouble with her mother. Racist or some fucked up thing. You know how those old-time families are. I think her real family was fucked up, too. It's a real mess."

He said, "You sure you don't want any blow?"

⟶⟵

Sometimes I think I know my cousin and I think she knows me.

Other times I think she's right to call us strangers.

"You," George the photographer snapped his fingers at Geri, at me. "And you. What's your name again?"

⤐⟨⟩⤏

My cousin never told me her birth name. The cop in the bar, when he said Geri found her real family—I didn't ask what he meant by that. My cousin never told me which of her own names, if she could choose, would feel most natural. She never said which life, if she could choose, she'd consider most real.

Lately Geri has been taking in orphans—crack babies, mostly—and stays up nights to rock them and sing to them and try to stop their crying. Some of the babies have names, some don't. Nearly all of them cry and go on crying and my cousin has to give them back to a system that might one day give them back to mothers who won't care if their babies go on crying or not.

"Some people should never have children," she says.

She says, "The important thing is not to get too attached."

She says, "There's not a whole lot anyone can do really."

She says, "I've never been good with kids."

Pretty soon, she will give up orphans and get a dog instead. She'll work the K-9 unit. Her dog will understand German and Geri will learn the words.

Uberfallen. Schneller machen. Guter hund. Jetzt ausruhen. Sicher. Guter hund.

Attack. Hurry. Good dog. Rest. Safe. Good dog.
More than once a dog will save her life, and vice versa.
"You can really trust dogs," she'll say.

19

Today I have to go to Boston, a trip for work.

I pack, kiss my kids, my husband. I'm not usually away from my family. I hate being away from my family, but I don't feel any of it because everything feels automatic. Lately I spend so much time thinking about family I've drifted from my own. Before I put miles between us, there are miles between us.

"Have a good trip," my husband says, and he doesn't look up from the dishes he's doing.

"Bye," Locklin says to the stove.

Phelan's the only one who seems like she'll miss me. She throws her arms open. She pretends to bawl. I think it's because she's watching an episode of *Barney* where Barney teaches Baby Bop what it means to be homesick. "It's good to have adventures," Barney says, and Baby Bop throws her lime-green self to the floor and pounds her fluffy dinosaur fists.

Despite everything, I don't think much about leaving until I'm already gone. Then I worry the way I always worry. I roll through movies of horrible things that will happen to everyone I love—faulty wiring in the basement, the stove left on, a stranger in the house. I call home. I call again. I say, "How's everybody?" I say, "I love you. I miss you. I'll be home soon."

Locklin says, "Bring me something."

Phelan says, "Present?"

My husband says, "Don't hurry back. We're fine."

❧

In Boston, I buy things. It's what I do when I'm upset. I learned it from my mother, whose moods my father could gauge by the number of new shoe boxes he'd find piled in the garage. I buy my family things to say I'm thinking of them. I buy them things to say I'm sorry. I buy them things to keep my mind off other things. I buy Locklin some Legos and a Thomas train. I buy my husband a baseball hat with a shamrock on it. I stop by a mall kiosk where a woman is selling Russian nesting dolls. I think these will be perfect for Phelan.

The woman selling the dolls has a Russian accent. I don't know how many of the dolls are authentic, how many of them actually came from Russia and not China, but right now the woman is sitting on a stool with her ankles crossed, at work on a small golden one. It could be a sales gimmick, but I stop to watch anyway.

The doll in the woman's hand looks a little like my daughter—blonde, rosy cheeked, green eyed—which means she looks like me, too, and probably like my sister and probably my birth mother and so on.

This is the way my mind works, a clock running backwards.

Soon I am not thinking of my daughter, how much she might love this doll, how much I miss and love her. I'm thinking this doll is a metaphor, a tiny sarcophagus, a little hollowed out self, and that it fits into another tiny sarcophagus, a series of tiny sarcophagi tucked into other sarcophagi, selves into selves, until they end with a larger self that looks whole but isn't.

I'd like to mail my birth mother this doll. I'd like to send her a note. I'd like the note to say, "I don't know how it is for you, but this is how it is for me." I'd leave out a doll or two, the smallest ones. I'd replace those missing selves with another note. It would be a simple note. "Fuck you," maybe.

⋘⟨⟩⋙

The doll's face is so intricate, down to the slivers of eyelashes, the flecks of light in her green eyes. It seemed beautiful a minute ago.

Now it's not.

"Sometimes we use needles to paint, very sharp," the Russian woman at the booth explains. "Must be careful," she says and shakes her hand like she's been pricked. She sticks a finger in her mouth. She sucks the imaginary blood.

⋘⟨⟩⋙

There are other nesting dolls, ones that are not blonde girls. There is a Jesus full of Jesus and another Jesus stuffed with the Holy Family, tiny Marys and Josephs and

119

three little wise men. There's Bo Peep and Boy Blue and an assortment of animal dolls.

Phelan likes penguins, so I buy a penguin doll. The penguins wear top hats and red bow ties. They have canes tucked in their wings like they are about to do a soft shoe. The tiniest penguin is the size of my pinkie nail. The details are perfect down to the nostrils on each beak.

"So lifelike. Almost real," the Russian woman says, as if bow-tied tap-dancing penguins were things found in nature.

❧❦☙

I bring the penguin dolls home and make a big deal out of them for my daughter. I open each penguin like a jewel box to reveal the next. Phelan squeals and claps. She covers her eyes and opens them again. Each time I pull out a new penguin I wave my hand and say, "Ta-da!" When we get to the smallest penguin, the fingernail sliver with the needle-pricked nostrils, she seems confused that magic like this could ever stop.

"More," she says.

"That's it," I say.

"More," she says.

I say, "That's as far as it goes."

Then I put the penguins back together, one into the other into the other, and start from the beginning. Each time we reach the end, Phelan is disappointed in the last penguin, that there isn't one more to discover, something else to know.

"What do you want to know?" the Catholic Charities counselor asked.

I said, "A medical history."

What else I wanted: a name for each doll-layer, each little box, each person inside a person inside me.

I keep the penguins high on a shelf in Phelan's room, out of reach, but somehow she gets hold of them. I catch her just as she puts the tiniest penguin in her mouth. I am frantic and fast. I turn her upside down. I whack her on the back, something I learned years before, a life saving technique, a glancing blow delivered right between the shoulder blades. The penguin goes flying out of my daughter's mouth.

It sails across the room right before she chokes on it.

20

When I hear from my birth family, it's e-mail again, this time from one of my two brothers. The subject line reads: BOOK.

In my first book, a memoir, I mention my birth name and my birth mother's name. These are names my parents told me, names I knew growing up. Both names are on my original birth certificate. My birth name is scrawled in Sharpie on my Catholic Charities file. These names are identifying facts, like my social security number and blood type and fingerprint. For most of my life I didn't think of my birth mother's name as attached to an actual person. I thought of it as a pin on a map, a mythological touchstone of a thing.

"I have read your book with interest," my brother writes.

⋘⟊⟊⟫

"Whose story is it anyway?" I ask students in my writing classes. All writing teachers have catchphrases they've learned from other writers and so on.

- A writer is someone who loves the names of things.
- Write to discover what you don't know.
- Write one true sentence and then write another.
- Your story is your story.

But there will be names people don't want spoken and discovery can be terrifying and the truth can mean different things to people and there are always other stories.

An adopted person's story is someone else's secret.

⨳

"You were my secret," Blonde4Eva said, and now I wasn't.

"Must be careful," the Russian dollmaker with the needle said, and held her hand over her mouth.

⨳

The Catholic Charities counselor held my file close. She pushed it across her desk, out of reach. Later, when she sent a report, she decided which parts of my story were mine to have. My birth mother's name, according to the report, wasn't mine to have.

Therefore I should un-know it.

⨳

My birth mother's name is such an ordinary one, as ordinary as *podium*, as *plant*, as *pen*. "Do you ever wonder about that?" Lucille Clifton wanted to know, how something plain could have so much power.

But in Grimm's fairy tale, Rumpelstiltskin demands the queen learn his name or lose her child. Ancient people believed to know someone's name was to know that person's essence. To change a name meant to change destiny.

The name I was born with means work and strain. The name I was born with was a wolf.

Lori is a laurel tree. Lori is a celebration.

A name can be a transformation or a cage, both.

⋞⊰⊱⋟

The man who says he's my brother knows about Blonde4Eva's e-mails and calls. He says he wants to open a different line of communication. He says his mother neither confirms nor denies who I am. He says his mother has gone on with her life. He says she does not want these memories. He says sorry. He says he doesn't mean to be blunt. He says maybe together we can figure this out. He signs his full name, a gesture of trust. He seems kind.

I examine his name. I examine his syntax. I look for a secret code in the formal tone—"with interest" and "neither confirms nor denies." It's what I did with Blonde4Eva, too. I consider the genetics of mid-sentence pauses, everything tentative, uncertain.

I consider comma splices.

Splice: to bring together strands, to interweave, to join segments of DNA.

"What do you think it means?" I ask my husband.

My husband is sick of me.

125

I know he's sick of me and I can't help it. I'm sick of me, too.

He says, "You are a sad little person."

I say, "I don't think it's an accident."

I say, "Everything means something."

"Stop it," my husband says, and goes back to the book he's reading. He reads on his belly, sprawled diagonally across our bed. Our bedroom is small. My husband is not. When he's reading, his feet block the path between the bed and the closet and I have to lift them, first one foot, then the next, to get by. Now I'm rougher than usual. I slap one foot up, then down. I do it again. Finally he says, "Don't take it out on me."

I say, "Who else is there to take it out on?"

Days later I write back and make plans to meet my brother. I don't think about what this might do to the families we both already have.

21

My brother and I talk on the phone before we meet in person. I take a Xanax and feel nauseous as I dial. I try standing, then I sit, then I stand again. I lean against the fireplace and stare at my husband's Myron Cope bobble-head. Myron Cope, the voice of the Steelers, the inventor of the Terrible Towel and the greatest sportscaster the Steel City has ever known, shakes his big Double Yoi head. "Hum hah," Myron would say, and only he would know what he meant.

After a few rings, my brother picks up. His voice is a Pittsburgh voice, like Myron's but softer, less metallic, not so much teeth grinding. It's a distinct working-class accent I've heard all my life and tried to escape.

Some things I don't know because adoption keeps things hidden.

Other things I don't know because I've worked to erase them myself.

"Not okel-dokel," Myron would say about that kind of erasing, but then he didn't know those boy cousins who used to push Geri and me face down on the sidewalk and make us kiss their feet. He didn't know the uncle who would grind his hips into mine at weddings and say it was o.k. because we weren't related, not really. "You're such a pretty girl," the uncle would say. "So blonde. How'd you get so blonde?" He didn't know the aunts who worried over my temperament, and the one who, after my grandmother died, kept saying, "Oh you remember my mother," as if my grandmother—who I bathed when she was sick and shared a bed with on vacations in Florida and loved the way any girl with a 250-pound Slovak grandmother who sang "My Ding-a-Ling" as a lullaby has ever loved any grandmother—had never been mine to love at all. Those kinds of Pittsburgh voices ruined that beautiful song for me, I thought maybe forever.

"Hey," my brother says, and his voice sounds like my father. His voice isn't as rough as Blonde4Eva's and I'm grateful.

"Well," he says. "This sure is something, am I right?"

"Hello," I say. I sound almost British, formal as a ticket. "It is."

◦⊰|⊱◦

"I can't believe this," my brother says.

I tell him I have a report from Catholic Charities. I tell him it's very detailed.

I want to say a report is not a life. I want to say a report is not a text to read backwards. I want to say something divided and divided can never be whole again. I don't say this because I don't want it to be true.

Instead I say, "It's hard to believe, I know."

128

"There were always stories," my brother says, "but who knows what's what."

On the mantle, Myron bobs his head, but his face looks confused. "I know what's what," Myron would say.

To my brother, I say, "I'm pretty sure what's in the report is right."

I tell him those stories.

22

ঙ্গ

Catholic Charities Non-Identifying Report: History
The birth mother's oldest sister reports that the birth mother is nervous and upset and hiding in a third-floor closet.

ఆ౹లూ

I'll call her Marie. Marie is not her name.

Marie is sweating. She huddles in the corner of the closet on a bed of old coats.

One of the coats is a rotted thing with a fox collar. It's the whole fox, head to tail, not just fur. The jaws are rigged to pop open and clamp down, so the body wraps itself like a scarf. One of the marble eyes is missing. The fox looks cockeyed, winking. Marie pops the fox's jaws open and closed to mark time. She runs her fingers along the edges where the teeth used to be.

ఆ౹లూ

It's December. The steam heat from the pipes hisses and clangs. Her belly is too large to hide. Marie is too large to hide. "Don't make a sound," her sister Eveleen says. "Don't let anyone hear you."

Marie knows she is an embarrassment. Eveleen tells her daily. Eveleen does not have to tell her. Marie has taken down the cheap full-length mirror here in this attic room so she doesn't have to see how embarrassing she is.

⋘⎮⎮⎮⎮⋙

"You look like Brigitte Bardot," the man who's made her pregnant said.

And she believed him! He had red hair, gawky, not even handsome enough to pull that line off. All Howdy Doody, really. He might as well have been wearing suspenders. He might as well have had a straw hat and been picking his toes.

What was she thinking?

Howdy Doody passed Marie a cigarette. She pretended to smoke it. He wore a pinkie ring. He carried a hankie. A hankie!

How could she have believed him?

She believed him.

And now she's the embarrassment.

⋘⎮⎮⎮⎮⋙

Downstairs there are visitors. They've come to see her poor sick niece with the bad heart, those beautiful blonde curls splayed on a pillow, the huge bandages over her chest. The child looks like a broken toy in that big bed. Of course people keep coming at all hours, bringing stuffed bears and casseroles and doing the little beauty's hair in ribbons and telling her how pretty she is, how she'll be back to her old self in no time.

"So good of you to come," a man's voice says.

This is code, her brother-in-law James. Each time she hears James' voice, each time there are footsteps on the porch, her heart pounds, her head rattles. If she's out, she climbs the stairs, pulls herself up by the hand-rail, and hides here, in the closet, with the mothballs and spiders she knows are everywhere even though she can't see them.

∽⊰⊱∾

She spends a lot of time in this closet now. It is becoming too much. Soon Eveleen will send her away, to a home for people like her, and she is almost happy for that. Her swollen ankles itch from the spider bites but her belly is so big it is impossible to reach down to scratch. She worries about the spiders. She worries they are poisonous. There is a type of spider, a brown recluse. It hides in closets like her. Indigenous, that's the word, and she thinks indigent, a welfare case. She wonders which word is most like herself. As for the spiders, their bites are dangerous. They leave ugly wounds that puss and bleed and open and keep opening like a secret that won't ever heal.

She thinks about these kinds of things, spider bites gone gangrenous, limbs cut off, when she hides in the dark and waits for people to leave.

"You worry about the wrong things," Eveleen says. "Look where that's gotten you."

⊷⊶

Marie puts a hand on her belly and rubs to stop the ache. She has always been such a thin woman. She has always been proud of this.

"You look real good in that green dress," Howdy Doody, whose other name she won't say now, said. He put his big farmer hand on her waist. He slid his hand up under her breast until she wriggled back. He said, "How about a cigarette?"

⊷⊶

She could never imagine being so big. She could never imagine being a mother, not like this, not shameful with this child, this *aberration* her mother would call it, if she knew, which she doesn't, thank God and Eveleen and James and the spiders and the one-eyed fox with the jaw that can't speak.

Marie's mother thinks Marie is off in Chicago.

Marie's mother thinks Marie has some fancy job in a typing pool.

"She is such a career girl," her mother brags. "Real modern."

Marie thinks of places she planned to go—Paris, mostly. When she was a girl, she'd cut pictures from magazines. The Eiffel Tower, the Arc de Triomphe, Tuileries.

134

She practiced pronunciations, pushing the air up and out her nose.

"Brigitte Bardot," Howdy Doody said, as if he'd known all along, as if he could read Marie's skin like Braille.

⋘⋙

Her father would throw Howdy Doody off a building.

Her father would beat this child out of her if he knew.

He does not know, will never know. The fox keeps its secrets.

Mistake, mistake, mistake. The word beats like a belt.

Sometimes Marie becomes her father and beats her own head, a fist to her temple, stupid stupid, until she gives herself such a headache.

"Aspirin's no good for a pregnant woman," Eveleen says.

Eveleen likes for Marie to suffer. Eveleen likes to remind Marie that the name Eveleen means "wished-for, longed-for child."

"Maybe one day you'll have a child you can name for me," Eveleen says and smiles down at Marie hiding here with the rotting fox and the filth and the spiders.

⋘⋙

That man.

He looks exactly like Howdy Doody. He wears cheap cufflinks with his initials on them. He looks like Howdy would look if Howdy Doody were a used car salesman.

Who would believe someone like that?

Who would believe a man with a hankie?

Marie believed they'd make a home, all tea towels and pillows and lace curtains on all the windows, like civilized people, like clean good people.

She is not clean good people.

"Confess," Eveleen says.

Marie took that cigarette. And now she has to hide away like this. She has to be careful not to walk on creaky floorboards. She has to know where to step.

ঔ{৹

The priest, what did he tell her?

"If you suffer, it's your own doing."

He said, "Do not bring shame to your family."

She is lucky Eveleen took her in. The priest told her that, too. She should be grateful.

These are the words everyone uses. Lucky. Grateful.

Maybe Marie is lucky, though her sister will wield this secret. Eveleen, who, longed-for or not, had not been their father's favorite, not the prettiest, not the smartest, but now look.

"Now look at you," Eveleen says. "You're lucky my husband is a good man. You're lucky, considering we have our own problems. Our poor little girl. She did nothing to deserve what's happened to her. Our girl didn't ask for what she got."

ঔ{৹

Marie knows she's asked for what she got, and so she says thank you when Eveleen gives her a pile of James' old work clothes to wear. She says thank you for the food they give her, even though she is often too sick to eat it. She hides what she can't eat. She tucks scraps in her pockets or leaves them in the closet. She is sure the scraps will bring mice along with the spiders. There are always smells to worry about, but Eveleen and James don't like waste.

The priest says, "You must honor your family."

⋘⋙

All Marie really wants is lemonade.

Before this, she hated lemonade. Now she wants gallons of it.

"You've always had fancy taste," Eveleen says, though what is fancy about lemonade? Marie makes it herself. James brings her old lemons from the sale produce rack at the grocery where he works. She squeezes them by hand, or she uses some of the cheap concentrate, though Eveleen sniffs at that and says it's too expensive.

"You always were one for the easy way out," Eveleen says.

Easy is a word they all use for her, too.

⋘⋙

Marie uses just a little sugar, not to be a burden. She likes the lemonade like that, not too sweet, more sour and bitter, almost metallic. It settles her stomach. The bitter taste

137

is the only thing that settles the baby, too, though she doesn't like to think of it like that, a baby.

Otherwise the thing just kicks and kicks all the time. It won't leave her alone. Just like its father, who followed her around with his cigarettes and his red hair and his promises. The baby, it, the baby it, kicks her ribs so hard Marie is sure they'll break. It kicks so hard it feels like it is trying to break through. It will never give her any rest unless she gives it lemonade and then, with that bitterness inside her, it will settle a bit.

Only then will it let her be.

23

The man who says he is my brother tells me stories he was raised on—rape, incest, an uncle come over from Ireland. He says those stories made the secret easy to keep.

He says everyone knew there was no rape. The truth—unspoken, forbidden—was probably something ordinary, a mistake.

A single young woman knocked up by a married man who wouldn't leave his wife.

A single young woman with old-world parents who would kill her if they knew.

He says his mother would never talk about it.

He says his mother will never talk about it.

He says she's difficult.

He says I can't imagine how difficult.

24

Catholic Charities Non-Identifying Report: Family Background
The birth mother provides a family history and reveals she never trusted anyone until the alleged birthfather and now she is sorry.

꧁༒꧂

This is years before, when Marie visits her father at work, after he's lost the leg.

She thinks it's funny that word, lost, like he left his leg somewhere with his keys and his glasses and his Iron City bottle opener. Her father is always losing something. He is always blaming her or the others for taking whatever he loses. Nothing is ever that man's fault.

"Now where have you damn kids put my this and put my that."

He goes on and on.

"I swear, I'll beat it out of you," he says, a promise he doesn't mind keeping.

He is bad-tempered. That's what her grandmother, her mam's mam, says. He is a spite devil, grandmother says, though who knows what that means. It sounds right.

He wakes up almost every day, smelly from beer and sleep-sweat, and starts ranting about what new thing has gone missing. Usually he ends up holding the thing he is looking for in his hand or he finds it later in his own pocket.

Marie thinks it is like that with a lot of things.

Everything people think they've lost is usually right there in their hands.

⋘∣∣∣⋙

The day she visits him at work, her father lost his lunch. Marie found it on the stoop when she went out for the mail. He must have set it down when he went to pet the dog. He always pets the dog goodbye. He forgets to hug his kids, kiss his wife, but the dog, that mangy old thing, he never forgets.

"Here Bangers," he says, "here boy," and her father scratches Bangers' ears and lets the dirty old thing kiss his face off.

He never raises his voice to the dog. He never so much as kicks the air between them.

"That dog's mouth is cleaner than yours," her father likes to say. Her father sticks out his tongue and lets Bangers lick it to show just how clean.

⋘∣∣∣⋙

Marie scoops up her father's lunch and walks 16 blocks to where he works in the city, at one of the office towers they're building. She doesn't know which company he works for. They all look the same. They all look dangerous.

"I'm in the danger business," her father says when he's been drinking. He makes guns with his fingers and shoots them in the air, pow pow. In life he works eight stories up, out on a beam, and fires a rivet gun, the sound of metal on metal.

From the ground her father looks small. She'd seen him work before, but never this high. Marie can't figure out how he balances like that, one wood leg, one good leg, both of them planted on a steel ledge no wider than her body. He can climb, too. He leads with his good leg, then uses one arm to hoist his wood leg up. He does this from beam to beam, almost graceful, almost like dancing.

Except it is not dancing.

Her father does not dance, even when he is very drunk.

"What do you think I am, a fool?" he says.

⋘∘⋙

No, not a fool.

Marie thinks her father looks like one of those plastic monkeys from a barrel, hands over feet over hands. My father, the monkey, the thought whips in her brain like a rope and makes her happy, as close as she ever gets to revenge.

Marie waits until her father makes his way down and ambles over to her. She sits on one of the spare beams. She waits a long time.

"What is it?" he says, in that clipped way he has.

"I brought your lunch," she says, clipped back.

He looks at the crumpled bag next to her on the beam.

"No need," he says. "I could've found something else. Head on back home before you're missed. Go on now, no place for you here."

No thank you. No hug or pat. No kiss like he gives the dog. He picks up the bag and hobbles off. The hinge of his wooden knee clicks as he steps.

❦

That's how it is and will forever be with the old man, the spite devil. They all fear and go on fearing him—she, her brothers, even her sister Eveleen, who is bigger than him and isn't above violence herself.

"Say it," Eveleen would say to their youngest brother when they were all still children. She'd hold his small face down in the dirt until he'd say the word that would damn him. "F-f-f-fuck," he'd say, with his stutter, his lisp. Then Eveleen would go tell their father, who would beat his son until his legs were covered in bruises, until it looked like he could almost shed his own skin.

Then, one day, their father turned and beat Eveleen, too.

Marie loves church because she should. Fear is another word for love, the priest says. In the Old Testament, the Commandments say honor thy father and mother. They say fear God. There's nothing about love. In church, her mother spends dollars they don't have to light candles and sends up prayers her husband will change.

He does not change.

Every night, he comes home, eats, gets drunk, unstraps his leg and sets it by the bedpost. Her mother massages his pink stump with oil.

⸻

The leg, left loose like that, looks like what it is—something cut from a tree. The foot has grooves where the toes would be, to make it more lifelike. Marie wonders if whoever made the leg signed it somewhere, the way sculptors sign their work. She wonders if maybe the legmaker meant something to be beautiful about it, but the leg frightens her like her father frightens her, so she never gets very close.

⸻

One time, when it was just the two of them in the house, Marie and her father, and he was almost sober, just a few beers in, when he was at the table, bent over the newspaper reading some stock reports about stocks he didn't own, she'd gone up to him. She'd pulled out a chair and sat down and told him she loved him.

He kept on reading.

She said, "Da?"

He kept on reading.

She said, "You want coffee? I'll make some."

He pushed his hair back on his head. It was greasy, unwashed, and so it stood up on one end like he'd meant to stick it there. It curved like a question mark.

He said, "Kellogg's is down three points. Who loses money on corn flakes? Everyone eats corn flakes. Corn flakes are a sure thing. Surest thing in the world."

She said, "Coffee, Da?"

He said, "There's nothing sure in this world. Remember that."

⇜⇝

Now she wonders if this is why what happened to her happened. She wonders, what's a girl to do when she grows up with a father like that?

She sure it's her fault after all. If she had remembered her father's advice, the thing that happened never would have happened.

Her father told her about the world. He told her not to trust anything.

He raised her not to believe in anyone, not even him.

25

My brother says his father was in the movie business. He says his father played piano. His father, my brother says, was an amazing piano player, long fingers, a real natural.

My brother wants to know if I play.

I tell him I do.

He says he hopes I'll play for him some time, and I tell him I will.

⋖⦙⦙⊳

Soon my brother and I will be together in my basement and I will play songs on the piano I learned on as a child.

The piano is over 30 years old, an upright Kimball, but the keys are good. My mother kept the wood polished with oil soap so it still shines. I do my best to keep it up. I polish it when I can.

I play my brother "Begin the Beguine," my father's favorite song. My father was a singer, before the war, before the mills, before he got bitter and sad and stopped singing. Once he won a contest and got to sing on the radio in Braddock, Pennsylvania, and for a while everybody knew him as the boy who sang on the radio. Then they forgot what song it was he sang. Then they forgot it was him who sang it. Then they forgot my father's name and how to spell it. Then they forgot my father ever sang at all.

The song he sang was "Begin the Beguine." The story goes, my father cut a record that day as part of his prize, but I never saw a record. No one did. My father must have kept it hidden or destroyed it. Or maybe there never was a record. Maybe that was just a story. Maybe there was just that one time in the radio studio, one take, the DJ picking his fingernails, saying, "This is it, kid. You got five minutes."

My father always thought the song's title was "Begin the Begin," as if any minute his life would start over, as if any minute it would be good.

I tell my brother this and laugh, even though I think it's sad.

It's one of the saddest stories I know.

⊷⊱⊰⊷

I play my brother another song—"Somewhere My Love," my mother's favorite, the theme song from *Dr. Zhivago*, a sap story set in the Bolshevik Revolution. I always hated this song. My mother would make me play it over and over for guests.

I tell my brother this story, too.

I tell him about the time my mother made me play it for her cousins, Dick and Stella.

"Dick was a bastard," I say.

"I know a lot of bastards," my brother says.

He says, "I know that's right," and puts a hand up for me to high-five.

⪻∘⪼

I'm 16 and Dick and Stella have just pulled up in their paneled station wagon. They're staying for the weekend. I hear Dick say, "Jesus fucking Christ," and I hear Stella apologize three ways.

I'm hiding out in my room when I hear my mother call, "Oh Lori baby. Come say hi to Dick and Stella. Come play 'Somewhere My Love' for us." It's her singsong, welcome-to-my-perfect-home voice.

My mother watches a lot of old movies. She's spent a lot of money on me—piano lessons, dance lessons, doctors, clothes and food. What she wants every once in a while is to impress people—in this case Dick and Stella. What she wants is for me to come out and be, just once, a perfect daughter. What she wants is a lacy white dress and pigtails and for me to say "Oh yes Mother dear." What she wants is for me to skip.

Most times I try. We keep our fights between us. In front of other people, I want her to be proud of me. I love my mother. I want to prove I haven't been a complete waste.

With Dick and Stella, though, there's a problem. Dick is nasty. He's also a drunk. He beats Stella. I do not know how often or how bad, but she is always nervous and he is always rough, and everyone in the family knows this and no one says much about it.

"You know how men are," the aunts say.

"They have a lot of passion between them," the aunts say.

"Dick has an artistic temperament," the aunts say, that word again, temperament.

I think Dick's name suits him. I tell my mother this.

"You will be respectful," my mother said before Dick and Stella arrived. "They're family," she said, as if that explained anything.

By artistic, the aunts mean Dick is a musician, a bar-room pianist, and a good one. When he plays, Stella sings along, like the terrified little lab mouse she is. Dick is not trained, like me. This, he reminds me each time we see each other, is important.

Trained pianists, Dick says, are like trained monkeys. Real musicians don't have to be taught how to run a scale or play the blues any more than real monkeys have to be taught how to swing from trees and fling shit.

"You're either born with it or you're not. Me, I never had one goddamn lesson," he says now as he settles into my mother's good wing-backed chair. He's wearing Hawaiian shorts and a tank top, black socks and sandals even though it's October, even though there's frost coming. He has a can of Iron City in one hand. The other hand keeps time to some music only he can hear. I think Dick is like a dog in this way. He's always hearing things. He taps out those rhythms on the arm of the chair. He rolls the beat through his fingers, like they're already on the keyboard, like they never can rest. I watch his fingers, how thick they are, how big and hard his hands seem. I imagine him hitting poor

Stella, those fingers coming down again and again in a slap. I can't imagine what she'd do that would make him so mad.

"My sweet Dick," she says, and her voice warbles and clicks, like a cotton candy machine filled with pennies. "He plays like an angel."

Maybe it's something awful and simple. Dick the angel-playing pianist can't bear the sound of his wife's voice.

"I'm a natural," he's saying. "I play by ear. Have since I was this high," Dick says, and he takes his rhythm hand down low, an inch off the carpet, to show he's been playing since he was a fetus.

Stella's tweaking, like a Pekingese on the 4th of July. When Dick tells her to get up to the piano, when he tells her to sing along to what I am about to play, she jumps like an M-80 just went off in her shoe. Poor Stella with the horrible voice sings when Dick says sing, even if he'll slap her for it later. I play my best for my mother, who wants to be proud, who wants to show me off, her well-trained and talented daughter. My mother sings along with Stella. They smile at each other as they sing. They hold hands, like singers do in those movies they watch. The two of them could torture dictators into giving up their countries, their families, their stashes of fine cigars, their own ears, they're so beautifully unimaginably off-key.

When it's over, Dick just sits in his chair.

"Well aren't you two the bee's knees," he says to my mother and Stella. He doesn't smile. His fingers thrum their invisible keys. He's quiet, then he says to me, "I can see you've practiced that one a lot."

I nod and think for a minute he's going to praise me.

He says, "You've been taking lessons for how long—three, four years now?"

He says, "How about I give it a go?"

He hoists himself out of the chair and walks to the piano like a linebacker. He sits down on the bench and it creaks under his weight. He rolls one wrist to loosen it, then the other.

Then he plays.

I'd like to say he's terrible. I'd like to say he hits the keys with a jazzy rendition of "Chopsticks." I'd like to say he thumps the keys like the brute he is.

But he plays beautifully. His fingers don't even seem to touch the keys. His whole body becomes part of the instrument, the music. There's no separating it.

Dick is a beautiful pianist and the world is worse because of it.

"There," he says when he is finished. "That's how a piano's meant to be played."

Weeks later, I'll get a letter from Dick, who will tell me I have the technical skill to be a concert pianist, but not the heart. I have the physical ability, but not the soul. I should give up and not waste any more time. "I figure I should tell you now for your own good," he says. "You are not a born pianist."

It's a crushing thing.

"You'll thank me," Dick writes.

❧

I didn't thank him that day. I didn't thank him ever.

I wished him dead more than once. I wished Stella

would kill him in his sleep—a pillow to the face, a stove left on, something easy like that.

Still Dick was right. I wouldn't become a pianist, though all these years later I still play, and one day I find myself sitting in the basement of my childhood home, playing the piano Dick once played, the very same piano, for a man who is my brother.

"You're really good," my brother says. "Just like my old man."

Maybe I wasn't born a pianist.

Maybe nobody's born anything, though Dick thought he was.

"I know a lot of dicks," my brother will say. "My father was one most of the time."

I won't know if my brother's father is my birthfather.

I won't be sure if it matters or not.

"Do you know any Bruce?" my brother will ask, and he'll mean Springsteen.

⋘∣⋙

Inside the Kimball piano, there are signatures. The man who tuned the piano when I was a child handed down his piano-tuning business to his son who handed it down to his. They handed down the tradition of signing the inside of the pianos, too. Every time one generation came to tune my piano, he saw the signature of the generation that came before him, a lineage of music, everything in tune.

"I've seen Bruce like forty times live," my brother says.

"I love Bruce," I say.

153

"We should go sometime," my brother says.

I say, "Definitely," though I'll probably never be able to afford tickets.

The last time the piano tuner called, I didn't call him back. The price went up. There were bills to pay. The kids needed things. Clothes. Shoes. Doctors' visits. The piano's out of key, but not too noticeable. You'd have to listen hard to hear what's off.

⥱⤫⥲

My brother says his childhood wasn't just movies and music.

It was tenements, motel rooms, a father who didn't come back when he said he would.

That father is dead now.

My brother says, "There are a lot of stories there, too."

⥱⤫⥲

When my mother asked me once too often to play "Somewhere My Love," I started to teach her to play it herself. I taught her the first ten notes. She'd plunk them out on the keys, awkward as an ice skater with a broken leg. That's as far as she got, those ten gimpy notes. Then she gave up. She'd play her ten notes, then collapse into a fist run down the keyboard. She'd do this every time she walked by the piano.

Now when I walk by the piano, I plunk out those horrible notes.

I don't visit my mother's grave very much.

But I long to hear her sing, that terrible, beautiful voice.

26

Catholic Charities Non-Identifying Report: Medical and Social History
The birth mother reports her relationship with the birthfather.

〜∞{∞〜

She will not allow herself to remember the songs.

Liars should be as easy to spot as redheads, as Howdy Doodys.

If Marie allows herself to remember, and she tries not to allow herself to remember, the songs were love songs and his hair wasn't really so red. It was more blondish, the red turning to gold under the club lights.

Straw into gold, Marie will think later, like her story is some child-story that doubled as a lesson. Rumpelstiltskin.

Love songs are pretty lies.

Rumpelstiltskin, if Marie remembers right, was a sneak and a cheat.

〜∞{∞〜

Howdy Doody is a sneak and a cheat. His eyes are the color of spring grass. That's what she thought when she looked into them, but of course she had been drinking, whiskey sours in fancy high-ball glasses. The cherries lulled around in the bottoms of the glasses. Slices of oranges were spiral-speared onto toothpicks that looked like swords. The cherries were pretty, even though she remembers thinking it's not good to eat those cherries because they're soaked in formaldehyde, like the bodies of the dead.

So there she was, looking at her pretty dead cherries and thinking about this man's spring-grass eyes and how handsome he looked in the club light, which is always misleading, that light. It's too dark, of course, but there's something else—all the rainbow colors from the floor lights and the mirror-ball lights make everything seem perfect when it's not. He held up one of those little swords, held it by its tiny handle between his big thumb and fore-finger. He had such large hands, he looked ridiculous.

It was all ridiculous.

He held the sword at her like that and held his other hand above his head like a fencer.

He said, "En garde."

Ridiculous! She should have taken that as a sign, she should have put her guard up and done like her father had taught her, but she didn't. She laughed. She thought he was charming. She thought he was a nice and charming man, so she held her own little sword up and clinked it against his.

When he asked her to dance, she did. He did not dance like a monkey. He was nothing like her father. He was smooth, like the floor was ice, like the world was ice, which it was. The world was that cold.

⚜

He wanted her to have the abortion. He knew someone, he said, someone who could do it cheap and keep quiet. It was nothing, just a procedure. Takes an hour, he said, two tops, then they could get back to their lives.

"What do you say?" he said. "Come on, B.B.," he said. "It's for the best."

⚜

He called her that, B.B., a nickname from that first time.

"You look like Brigitte Bardot," he'd said. "I want to take you to Paris. We'll stand on the Eiffel Tower. Did you know it's so high you're in the clouds? You can look down and see airplanes at your feet. You'll be like King Kong."

No, not like King Kong.

Like her father, the monkey, dancing his sick dance, hundreds of feet above the ground.

⚜

What this man, this liar, wanted her to do—live with him.

"Go on. Have it if you want," he said. "Just stay with me."

He offered her an apartment, not a house. He didn't have much furniture. Marie imagined tea towels and lace

159

curtains. She imagined a real bed and couch. He did not say marry me. He did not say anything about forever. He said something about soon.

Eveleen, of course, found him out. It was in the paper, divorce proceedings. He was already married, which is why he did not say marry.

He already had a child, which is why he does not want this one.

❧

His child is six years old. Marie tries to imagine a six-year-old child. She tries to imagine walking away from that.

She sees her niece with the bad heart, lying in bed, her chest torn open, the bloodied bandages, asking her mother why it hurts so much.

❧

Of course he comes back and offers to marry.

"I did it for you," he says about the divorce.

He asks Marie to keep the baby.

"If you don't want to raise it, I will," he says, too late.

❧

Some days Marie thinks of Paris, escaping there, the Eiffel Tower, planes passing by. She thinks of her father on top of those skyscrapers, all those clouds beneath his one good foot.

27

Catholic Charities Non-Identifying Report: Residency and Birth

The birth mother reports she is unnerved.

⊷❦⊶

The place Eveleen finds for Marie is called Rosalia, little rose, for Mary, the virgin mother. Marie has never understood that part of the story. She reads the Bible, but the words are confusing. She listens to the priest who explains the part about the angel, the divine pregnancy, but no one talks about how Mary explained things. What did she tell Joseph? What did she tell her family? What did she do with all that shame?

"Look at yourself," Eveleen had said when Marie first came to her.

As Marie grew and kept growing, Eveleen offered up her husband's clothes, an ace bandage for Marie to wrap around her belly, girdles so tight Marie's back and legs went numb.

"Cover that up," Eveleen says, the disgust like mud on her tongue, but there is no covering anything now.

At Rosalia, they give all the girls—that's what the nuns call them, girls—navy blue dresses that hang loose so they all look like bells with the clappers torn out. They walk the halls, hands on their ridiculous bellies, heads down, waddling this way and that.

Marie imagines a sound, the clanging, a chorus, all those fat sad bells.

"What happened to you?" one of the girls, Samcie, asks Marie on her first day, but Marie doesn't bother to answer, the question is that stupid.

Stupid Samcie, with her fat face covered in dark spots, the mask of pregnancy—that's what the nuns call it, its proper name, a mask—spread across her cheeks and eyes. Samcie looks like a raccoon, only raccoons are smart. Raccoons can take the lids off garbage cans and open doors, open a bag of potato chips even, feed themselves in the streets.

Raccoons would never find themselves in a place like this.

But here is Marie, and here is Samcie, and here they all are, these girls who trusted men and spread their legs for them and took in their promises and their cocks and ended up in this place named for a virgin, such a horrible joke.

There is a huge statue of Mary out front, and tiny statues of her everywhere inside—little virgins on windowsills, on the backs of toilets, in the library, which isn't much of a library, just one shelf with some bibles and inspirational guides to clean living. Marie wonders if the irony is on purpose, all these virgins in a home for unwed mothers. Even nuns are not that cruel. Then again, Marie grew up in the church with her parents and their parents and so on. She knew cruel.

"Look," the statues are meant to say. "This is what a good mother looks like."

The statues say, "You can pray to us for salvation because we are what you'll never be."

Marie's only salvation: she knows her time here won't be long. Her room isn't bad. A single bed, a crucifix, a closet to hang the navy bell dress in, no mirrors.

"A blessing," Eveleen would say.

∽⊰⊱∾

Marie will wait one month exactly before it comes. She'll be afraid of things—her water breaking, for instance—but when it happens, she'll think she's had an accident. It will be just a little water at first, a trickle. When the contractions start, they will be drunk fists deciding whether or not to fight, opening and closing, anger and release. Marie will call for Sister Beatrice, the kindest of the nuns, the one who always brings Marie juice when she is too tired and sore to get up and get it herself. Sister Beatrice will bend over Marie's bed. She will lift the blue bell dress. She will press on Marie's stomach and the rest of the water will come forward, a sloshed bucket. Marie won't feel anything, but she will hear the water splash on the floor, see it wet Sister Beatrice's nice black shoes.

Marie is embarrassed by this.

"I'm sorry," she says to Sister Beatrice.

"It's nothing," Sister Beatrice says. "Just be calm now. It will be over soon."

The hospital is connected to the home. Sister Beatrice gives her something soothing. It tastes like cherries. Marie remembers the cherries in the drinks she had that night that feels a long time ago, cherries in the whiskey sours, cherries soaked in formaldehyde, the drink of the dead, how sweet the cherries were, how she knew she shouldn't have eaten them.

She says again, "I'm sorry about your shoes," and Sister Beatrice says, "Just be quiet now."

Marie is quiet. She tries to be good. She had been a good girl once. Her mother had always been proud of her. Her mother had lit candles in hopes her father would change. Her mother believed change was possible and maybe it was.

The candles her mother lit were red, the color of cherries.

Nothing is cherry now.

※

The baby is born broken, its legs mangled, but someone else will come and fix it, people with money. People who have love in their hearts, enough for a broken baby. Marie holds the little girl, then lets it go. She's allowed visits, but she won't ever hold it again. She won't pick it up.

She'll touch its arms, its belly, but never the legs, and she won't cradle it again.

There is no sense in naming it, but it seems wrong to let a baby lie there broken, its legs going this way and that. It seems wrong that they'll have nothing to call it in the meantime, before the rich people come. The nuns will care for it. They have to call it something. They will judge Marie even more harshly if she doesn't give it a proper name, and so Marie names it Amelia. Born February 6, 1964 at 11 a.m., weighing 7 lbs. 9 oz., 19 inches long.

Marie thinks Amelia is a proper name.

⌐⊙{⌐⊙⌐

Sister Beatrice gives Marie a pill to dry up the milk. Marie's breasts hurt. They feel hot and bruised all over. She thinks about milk drying up, a puddle in the sun, a milkshake, a long straw, someone sucking her dry.

"You could choose to nurse the baby, if you want," Sister Beatrice says. "It would help with the pain."

But she can't bear that, either, that broken baby's mouth on her. Its legs remind her of her father, that twisted crippled monkey.

"Sin begets sin," the priest would say.

She can't bear to hold it when she stops by the crib to look. For a while that's what she calls it—It. She feels guilty about that, too.

⌐⊙{⌐⊙⌐

In a few days her milk dries up, as Sister Beatrice promised, and her body is empty and new again and she feels almost herself. Marie lights candles and pays a dollar each time from the money Eveleen sends with notes that say, "I hope you know what a sacrifice it's been."

28

ঙ

My parents told me a lot of stories about myself.

One of their favorites was about the day they adopted me.

"The nuns brought you out in a pretty pink dress that covered your leg brace," my mother said. "You were such a happy baby."

My father said, "You didn't make a peep. You didn't even cry at all."

My mother said, "On the car ride home, you just stared and stared at your father. You loved him right away."

Born crippled, I spent a lot of time in hospitals. When visiting hours were over and my father had to leave, the stories went, I'd scream for him. My cries would echo down the hall as my father walked out. He could hear them in the elevator shaft. Sometimes he thought he could hear me calling for him out in the hospital parking lot.

"I thought you'd explode," my father said.

"The lungs on you," my mother said. "People think babies always want their mothers, but not you. It was like your father was all that mattered to you. Like I didn't exist at all."

⁓⦑│⦒⁓

On the day my parents bring me home, they take a picture. The picture is black and white. I'm sitting in the grass in a lace dress. My head seems big for my body. I look like a bobblehead, a mini Myron, a cartoon baby. It looks like the weight of my own head will topple me. My father takes the picture. I can tell because his shadow is there in the photograph. His legs are two skyscrapers. I'm looking up.

The first time I go to New York City, a friend will warn me, "Whatever you do, don't look up." She means it will confuse me. She means I'll look like a tourist. She means if I'm not careful I'll get mugged.

⁓⦑│⦒⁓

In the photo my father takes, I'm squinting. My face is scrunched. I don't look upset. I look like I'm weighing things. I look like I'm figuring out an equation. I look confused.

⁓⦑│⦒⁓

"I knew right away you were smart," my father always said.

But when he was angry, he'd say, "You think you're so smart, smart ass. Little Miss College. I have more brains in my ass than you have in your whole body."

168

There are stories my parents told about their own lives.

Those stories became my stories and stories became my life.

⤜❦⤛

My parents' story about the day they met goes like this:

My mother is in her dress uniform from nursing school, wool cape flapping behind her. She wears Sani-White shoes and white stockings. Her hair is black as a crow's wing.

My father is just back from the war, a new pack of Pall Malls in his chest pocket, a gold ring on his pinkie. A wave of hair crooks across his forehead like a finger.

Their paths cross on the Main Street sidewalk, Braddock, PA.

My mother's cape brushes my father's arm. His arm is thick, muscled. He's taken a job at Iron City Beer. He throws cases of beer onto a beer truck. He drives the truck, loads, unloads. He looks like the kind of man who'd do a job like that, a sailor who hasn't stopped being a sailor.

"She wouldn't give me the time of day," my father said and he looked at his wrist where there wasn't a watch to read.

Back on the sidewalk, my father whistles. He catcalls. He falls down in front of my mother, who steps over him, dainty, in her spotless white shoes. He rolls around and grabs his chest like he's dying. His tongue lolls out. He plays dead. He says he can't get up, will not get up, until this beautiful woman in the perfect shoes and white stockings and skirt, a skirt he can almost look up from where he's lying, gives him her phone number. He says he will die, right here on this very sidewalk, if he can't get her number.

He says he means it.

He says he's never meant anything more in his whole life.

"What could I do?" my mother said. "I gave him my number. He wrote it on his arm like a crazy person. Like this guy we had in the psych ward who put his pants on backwards so we girls wouldn't be afraid of him. Like backwards pants meant he was safe. This psych guy, he couldn't remember his own name. He wrote it over and over, up and down his arms and legs. Your father wrote my number down, just like that. And then he called and called until I agreed to go out with him."

My father nodded. He smiled at my mother, the most beautiful woman he'd ever seen.

"And I've regretted it ever since," my mother said.

∽❦❧∽

My father died.

Then my mother died.

"First one goes, then the other," the funeral director said when he buried my father.

The betting odds for funeral directors on such things is five years, tops. Funeral directors, my friend Adam says,

170

really do take bets, like mortality is a lottery everyone has to play. Adam writes obituaries for the local daily paper. He goes to the Christmas parties funeral directors throw every year. Adam says the parties are a lot of fun. Polkas, raffles, bingo, etc. Adam says people who deal in death know how to drink.

⮜❦⮞

My mother made it almost five years. After her funeral, her friend Pauline sent me a letter and a picture. "Thought you might want this," she wrote. "It's from the night your parents met."

There are three couples in the picture.

One couple I don't recognize.

The other two I do.

⮜❦⮞

Pauline is on a date with my father.

My mother is on a date with someone else.

In the picture, my father's dressed sharp—wire-rim glasses, a print tie, white shirt with the cuffs rolled back, hair gelled into that heartbreaker, finger-hook wave. Pauline leans into him, smiling, adorable in a pretty flowered dress.

They look like they're having fun.

My mother is having fun, too. She smiles—a bigger smile than I've ever seen on her. She wears a peasant shirt and I remember her telling me when I was very young that she liked these shirts. She called them gypsy shirts. She said people in my father's family called her a gypsy because she was very dark skinned and liked bright lipstick and smelled like the garlic her mother made her smear on her toast every morning. She said my father's family was afraid she'd put a curse on them. She said that was the only reason they were ever nice to her.

Fear did that, she said. It wouldn't make people love you, but it would make them polite. My mother seemed to like that.

But this moment in this picture is before all that.

Here my mother is simply beautiful in her white gypsy shirt and she's three people away from my father. Her date looks bored. He stares off, away from the camera, like there's something dreamy just a few feet over if he could just get away from these ridiculous people.

Pauline ends up marrying him.

My mother ends up with my father.

Pauline's letter doesn't explain how that happened. She doesn't explain why my parents invented a movie version of their meeting.

"People believe what they need to believe," my mother told me, but she was talking about religion, about how people told themselves stories so they could keep going even though they knew the truth about things—that there's so little we can do for each other in this life, that everyone we love dies, no matter what.

29

ई

My brother says Blonde4Eva does not represent the family. He says it's important I understand this. He says, "We have two brothers, two sisters." Only one, he says, is Blonde4Eva. Our other sister, he says, is a lot like him. Our other brother is a lawyer.

My brother apologizes for that.

He says "seriously."

He says I should be happy.

He says I should be grateful.

He calls me lucky.

He says I should imagine his growing up, the deadbeat piano playing father, his mother, her troubles. He says he almost wishes my story had been his story.

He calls me Amelia, as if this has always been my name.

30

My brother and I agree to meet at a place called Fat Head's on Pittsburgh's South Side. I tell him I'll wear my green coat.

"Like Oscar the Grouch green," I say, "Easy to spot."

"Do you always dress like a Muppet?" my brother says and sounds serious, maybe worried.

We know so little about each other. The whole thing feels off, an internet date.

My friend John, a smoker with a pit bull, lists "hula hoops and walks in the rain" as his Likes on Match.com. What John really likes are hamburgers and Marlboros and getting blown in movie theatres by women in their twenties.

"There's nothing wrong with a little self-invention," John says. When John goes on dates, he ditches his usual t-shirts. He wears a black turtleneck, a tweed blazer, and, in winter, a cashmere scarf. He carries a rose. He tells women he's an artist who's big in Japan.

"You are what people think you are," my mother said.

"No," I say to my brother. "Sometimes I dress like a mime." Then I say, "I'm kidding." Then I say, "No, really."

I don't ask my brother how I'll recognize him.
I think I'll know.

31

My husband and I leave the kids with a sitter.

"Where are you going?" Locklin asks. He's on the floor in the living room playing Legos. He holds two Lego spaceships, one in each hand, and crashes them, pow pow.

"Fire!" he yells. "Help!"

Bits of Lego go flying, tiny plastic projectiles.

I say, "Be careful. Watch your eyes."

Locklin rolls those eyes and says, "Mom, you worry too much," in a voice that ages him into his teen years.

When I tell my son we're going to meet someone, he wants to know who.

When I tell him it's a brother I never knew I had, he wants to know why.

"Is it important?" he asks.

I say, "I think so, maybe."

Locklin knows a little of my story and the way it connects to his own story. He already likes the idea of family history, lineage. He asks me over and over to tell about when he was born, how the nurse, impressed by his wailing, said, "Listen to the lungs on this one." He likes me to tell him how his father and I wept when we first saw him, we loved him so much. He likes me to describe the way we all passed out together in the hospital room, all of us snoring and drooling.

Locklin has seen enough Disney to understand the word *orphan*.

"Why do all the mothers die?" he wants to know.

He's seen a lot of movies that help him make sense of the world, or not.

Locklin thinks for a minute, looks at the ragged remains of his spaceships, and says, "Oh, like *Star Wars*. Luke and Leia," then he goes on crashing.

⋞⟊⟊⟊⟊⟊⋟

My father called me *princess* but I'm not royalty.

Luke was a farmer's son.

I am a mill worker's daughter.

Not Luke and Leia.

Two Lukes, maybe.

32

On the drive over the 10ᵗʰ Street Bridge, I think I might throw up. I rub the sleeve of my mossy Muppet coat, back and forth, until it shines.

"Be good to each other. Love and forgive everybody." Jim Henson's advice.

To my husband I say, "I think my brother will look like me, don't you?"

I say, "I hope he's not an asshole."

I say, "I hope he'll give me the medical history."

I say, "A medical history's important."

I say, "This is a good idea, right?"

⋘∙⋙

I take half a Xanax and hope it calms me down.

"Be careful drinking on that," my husband says.

I say, "A half won't hurt," then I take the other half.

I don't realize I'm shaking until I get out of the car and try to load the parking meter and the quarters fall to the curb. I've brought a copy of my Catholic Charities report in a manila envelope. I keep it tucked tight under my arm as I try to gather the quarters up. I think of the report as credentials, proof that I am who I say I am, a passport.

My husband wiggles the report free. He bends down and helps me pick up the quarters. He feeds the meter. He kisses me hard on the head, his lips in my hair, on my forehead, as if I were a child, which is exactly how I feel.

He says, "This will be great or it won't, don't worry, we'll get drunk and sneak away, no matter what. You're fine. You're loved." He holds me with one hand and explains our love with his other hand. "This," and he moves his finger through the air, connecting dots, his face to my face and back to his, "is what matters. This is your family, right here, between us, what we make." Then he says, "You'll understand better when I fuck you tonight."

I love him very much.

❧❦❧

Inside Fat Heads, it's Happy Hour. People press to the front window and belly up to the bar. The Fat Heads logo—a giant cartoon head, bald, three chins, a dust-broom mustache and Ray Bans—floats above every-thing. Fat Head is on the walls, the windows. He looks like John Belushi on a booze-and-Oreos bender. He looks like something out of Orwell. Big Brother with Type 2 diabetes, watching. Fat Head is a drunk uncle who sneaks beer to children.

"The wait's an hour. Table for two?" the hostess in the pink muscle shirt asks.

I say, "That's o.k. We're meeting somebody."

"Take a look around then, see if you can find them," she says. She blows her bangs out of her eyes and rubs the back of her neck with one hand. She turns back to her clipboard. Fat Head hovers on her shirt, right above her lovely boobs, along with the words "Kiss Me I'm Foamous."

⚜

My brother spots me first. It's the coat, I'm sure, but then I remember my book, the pictures of me that have been in local papers, and I realize my brother knows more about me than I realized, more than I know about him.

"Hey!" he shouts and throws an arm up.

He is tucked behind a wall. The table in front of him is filled with empty beers, a few half-full ones. There are two women with him. I think the three of them have been here a while.

As I come closer, my brother seems tall, long-limbed, even though he's seated. His hair is brown, the color mine would be if I didn't dye it blonde. His eyebrows are thick and high-arched. They make him look surprised. He seems happy, sweet, with a loopy crooked grin that makes him seem much younger than a man approaching middle age. His hair is close cropped, with bangs that make him look like a boy on the first day of school. He also looks a little drunk. His eyes are shiny. His shirt collar is crooked. He seems nervous.

He half stands, then wipes his hand on his pants be-

181

fore he reaches to shake mine. I introduce my husband and my brother introduces the woman to his left as his wife. She wears a fur-collared sweater and smudged eye makeup. She looks angry, like she's been dragged here, like she's barely tolerating this. She has a Coke in front of her, a half-eaten sandwich, and it's clear she doesn't approve of the beer my brother has been drinking, especially the one he almost topples when he sits back down. It's clear she doesn't approve of any of this. She knows things I don't. Maybe she's right to be angry.

"It's always great to meet another member of my husband's family," she says, and her sarcasm is its own limp wet hand.

My brother seems to not hear her, or he's used to this. He introduces the other woman, who is across from his wife and her exact opposite, yin to yang, all smiles and light. She's blonde and looks a little like me—same eyes, eyebrows, cheekbones. She keeps tucking her hair behind her ears and I notice the lobes, thick, sturdy.

It's an odd thing to notice, someone's ears.

My mother's ears were so tiny, they looked like doll's ears. Mine are large, fleshy. It was one of the many visible differences between us. "Be happy you can wear earrings," my mother used to say. "I don't have anything to pierce."

This sister with ears like mine is not Blonde4Eva. When she says Blonde4Eva's name, she nods and my brother and his wife nod back and I wonder again if Blonde4Eva might be dangerous. They nod like this when they mention my birth mother, too.

"You might have heard. Mommy's very old school," my sister says.

My brother's wife squints and says, "You've got that right."

My brother's wife takes a drag on her Coke. She says, "That's one way to put it."

My sister goes on as if nothing just happened. "This explains so much. You being born and all. I think this will help. I think it would be good for them to meet, don't you?" she says to my brother, our brother, who shrugs. "I think it would really help," my sister says.

She looks at me as if I should understand.

❦

"Well, this is really something," my brother says, and he stares at me and goes on staring. I'm not sure what he sees, but whatever it is, he seems stunned, like someone caught at a busy intersection, unable to cross the street.

I'm the star of my own movie. My brother is the star of his. My birth mother is the star of hers. We are all the stars of our own movies, the only ones worthy of a close-up.

When I imagined this moment, I imagined it from one angle. I imagined the way I'd experience it. This would be the moment I'd finally see people who were related to me. The camera would zoom in on that—my face, their faces, my face.

My face.

I thought of this moment as a kind of funhouse mirror, maybe—something that could show me myself in

183

new unexpected ways. But it was always about me. I never thought what it would be like for the others. I never considered them in their own close-ups. I never thought what it would be like to be the mirror.

"Hold out your hands," my sister says, and I'm not sure what she wants.

She holds up her hands, palm out. My brother puts one of his hands against hers. He holds his other hand up to me. I don't know what else to do, so I put my hands against theirs, these two strangers, and we measure them. All three of us have big hands, long fingers, squared off at the tips, piano players, construction workers.

"Everyone in our family has big hands," my sister says.

She says, "So how are your teeth?"

⌒⟨⟩⌒

We all drink a lot, everyone except my brother's wife, who looks miserable. We talk about things that are family. We talk about things that are not family. We move down the street to Jack's Bar. The sign out front says: A Pittsburgh Legend, over 18,400,000 served, Open 365 Days a Year.

We play pool. We eat two-for-one hot dogs. We drink more. We drink more. We drink until it all feels natural, until my sister calls my husband her favorite brother-in-law and my brother gets in a scuffle after he whacks some guy in the butt with his pool cue and my sister puts up her dukes, does a bob-and-weave and says, "Beer fists."

⌒⟨⟩⌒

Both my brother and sister think of themselves as Irish, even though it's just their mother's side and their last name is very German.

"Good Irish boy," my brother calls himself.

"I'm a good Irish girl," my sister says.

I think of my friend Sinead, the Irish accountants, what they'd all make of this.

"Jesus Mary and Joseph," they'd say.

"Americans with their tennis shoes," they'd say. "Think they can run over everything."

Neither my brother nor my sister has been to Ireland. One has a map of Ireland tattooed on a calf. The other has a shamrock on a shoulder. My brother's wife has a sun tattooed on one arm and pulls back her sweater to show it. I have a couple tattoos of flowers. One is a lotus. Lotuses stay rooted, but float, too. I try to explain this, what it means to me, but the truth is I got all my tattoos when I was drunk and they're not all that meaningful.

As for the lotus, I was allergic to the ink. The petals are still swollen, faded. It looks like I was tattooed with puffy paint. It feels like a tattoo in Braille.

"We should get matching tats," my brother says. "We should get the family crest. Right here," he says, and rolls up a shirt sleeve to show his forearm, right beneath the crook of his elbow, a very painful and allergy-inducing spot for a tattoo.

⋘∣⋙

I have that beer-coaster copy of the family crest, the one Sinead sent me a long time ago. I want to tell my brother and sister this, but I don't. I want to joke that getting a tattoo in the shape of a beer coaster might be a practical thing, considering how much we are all drinking, but I don't say that either.

There are a lot of shamrocks in Jack's Bar. There are signs for Bushmill's and Jameson's and Smithwick's. There's a sign that reads: "An Irishman Gets More Irish the Further He Gets from Ireland."

Being Irish in America is an excuse to drink a lot.

Being Irish in America is often a pass to be an asshole.

St. Patty's Day parades in America are traditionally homophobic and racist, so much so that one day Guinness will pull sponsorship from the New York City parade. "Guinness is an advocate for all," the company will say. "We believe in diversity."

"Guinness is good for you," the beer billboards in Ireland say.

I've been to Ireland many times, on layovers when I worked for the airlines and then to see Sinead in Galway. In Ireland, I saw maybe two black people and no openly gay people. The bars close at 10 p.m. and hairy bouncers grab whoever's near them at 9:59 and start muscling out. The first time this happened to me, I wanted to fight, like beer fists might be a genetic thing. I'd had two beers, wasn't drunk, and didn't understand.

"It's not personal," Sinead told me. "They're just grabbing whatever's close. They're paid to jack."

The first time we were jacked, Sinead and I fell into a British guy who, when he found out I was American, was excited.

"I fancy Wu-Tang very much," he said. "Do you fancy the Wu-Tang?"

It was weird to hear someone talk about American gangster rap like it was all grandfathers with peppermints. Here, would you fancy one? Now isn't that refreshing?

It's hard to know what you're born with and what you take in as you go.

∽ଡ଼|ଡ଼∽

Sinead knows when a fight is a born one. She knows what's personal, I think.

Her grandfather was a driver for Michael Collins and the IRA.

"Americans come over in their green t-shirts and think being Irish means little green men and green beer," she'd say. Then she'd pat my leg and say, "Not you, of course. I mean the other Americans," though of course she meant me.

∽ଡ଼|ଡ଼∽

In Jack's, I put The Pogues and Van Morrison and Christy Moore on the jukebox. I pound a table. I sing along to "Fairytale in New York." My brother high fives me and says, "Good Irish girl." I want to fit in. I'm happy to feel like I fit in.

My brother toddles off to the bathroom. His poor wife sits at the bar, picking at the matted fur on her collar and checking her phone. My sister flirts with a bald biker guy who leans over her as she lines up a shot at the pool table. When she scratches, she giggles and rubs the biker's head. "For luck," she yells, and makes a big show of chalking her cue, then blowing the extra powder off the tip.

"At least we see where you get your love of booze," my husband yells into my ear and we clink glasses.

We take a lot of pictures. My husband snaps shots of the three of us, me in the middle, my brother and sister towering over me like bookends.

"Smile and say family," my husband says.

In the morning, I'll have a bad hangover, shortwave static in my eyelids, beer fists in my brain. I'll look at the pictures and search our faces to find every little like-thing.

ᵉᴳ{)ᵒ

My brother sends me home with other pictures, too, pictures of my birth mother and the rest of the family. My birth mother looks like anyone. I could have passed her for years on the street and not noticed. She looks like a regular at the bingo hall. She looks like someone else's mother. I don't know why this is shocking but it is.

"She looked exactly like you when she was young," my brother says.

My birth mother's dyed blonde hair is short. She wears big glasses. She wears pant suits, polyester-looking outfits. She's very thin, "from the cancer," my brother

188

says. She has a stoma. She keeps it covered with gauze, sometimes a scarf.

"She still smokes. Can you believe that?" my brother says, and holds his own cigarette to his throat to demonstrate how. "She's that stubborn," he says. "She's a tough Irish woman." He sounds proud of this.

I don't know what he means by tough Irish woman. My Irish friends are kind, gentle people. When my father was dying, Sinead called me every day from Galway. This was back when long distance meant something, when there were phone bills to worry about, when the world was a much bigger place.

Other than the stoma, my birth mother looks completely unexceptional, tough or not. She looks as ordinary as her name. I've imagined many things about my birth mother. I never imagined ordinary. Of all the things my own mother was, of all the things I've said and thought about her, ordinary was not among them.

"There is no such thing as an ordinary life," I tell my students. I tell myself this, too. I believe this. I quote Walt Whitman. "I am large. I contain multitudes." I quote Charlotte the spider. "We're born. We live a while. We die."

I see the miracle of that. I understand we're all a punchline.

My birth mother has a perm.

⚜

I believe a lot of things because it's better to believe them than to believe their opposites.

My parents thought I'd been born gifted. They told me I was beautiful, always. They entered me in beautiful baby contests, modeling contests, a beauty pageant once, and even though I always lost, I believed them. They loved me enough to make me believe I was beautiful. The truth is I have one of those faces people don't remember. It's passable, pleasant enough.

I've had a lot of perms.

⁓◦{}◦⁓

"You need something to make you stand out," one of my roommates in New York used to tell me. She was a hairdresser. She worked at Vidal Sassoon. Sometimes she'd use me as a hair model. She liked to experiment. One time she gave me a cut that made me look like Andy Warhol. People remembered me for a while then, because of the cut, and the red lipstick I wore with it. The lipstick color was called Savage Rage. My roommate made a big deal out of reminding people that Andy and I were both from Pittsburgh, which is why I looked so much like him. "The Factory," hipsters at The Cat Club would say. "I get it."

Then my hair grew and I went back to pink lipstick and I was ordinary again.

⁓◦{}◦⁓

"She looked just like you when she was young," my brother says of my birth mother.

Blonde4Eva looks ordinary, too. Heavyset. Dyed blonde permed hair to match her mother's. In the picture my brother gives me, she's wearing a bright Christmas sweater, an embroidered reindeer with jingle-belled antlers across the front. She does not look dangerous. She looks like what she is—someone's mother, someone's sister, my sister, one of my sisters.

Some of the pictures were taken in a church. My birth mother is in the middle, surrounded by her children. Two of them kneel in front of her. Off to the left, there's an icon, the Virgin Mary. There are flowers at her feet, so I think this is a Feast Day or Mother's Day. The way she's seated, my birth mother looks like her own kind of icon—all bone-straight posture, flat expression, feet and knees prim together, hands folded, prayer-like, on her lap. I imagine a snake crushed beneath her sensibly-shoed feet, her four legitimate children bowing down and bearing gifts.

⋞⟨⟩⟫

When I ask my brother if he thinks she'll give in, if he thinks she'll give me a medical history, considering the cancer and all, he says, "Be patient. Let me handle this."

He says, "She's not good with strangers."

He says, "Are you nervous?"

He says, "Are you paranoid?"

He says, "We get that from Mommy."

33

My husband and I get home at 3 a.m. and pay the sitter, who charges us double after midnight and leaves the house trashed.

"Somehow he ate the whole package of Oreos," the sitter says about Locklin.

The empty package of Double Stufs is on the living room table. There are crushed Oreos all over the rug and Oreos ground into the arm of the couch the sitter sprawls on. There's a half-empty bag of Goldfish, too, and orange Goldfish dust is everywhere, along with crushed juice boxes that were squeezed like squirt guns all over the house. Everything's sticky.

"Yeah, she wanted crackers," the sitter says about Phelan.

The sitter's name is John. John's got the TV tuned to MTV, some reality show, which seems funny right now because I feel like I'm in one.

John's a terrible sitter, an old student with a mangy goatee and hipster glasses, but we don't have many options. He likes our kids and they like him and John keeps them safe. Most of the sitters in the neighborhood want a regular schedule. We don't have a regular schedule. We don't go out much. We try to juggle our work schedules so one of us can be with the kids while the other's working. Our idea of a good time is to nap. When we're lucky, we get to sit at our kitchen table, eat and drink with each other, talk to each other, write books, have sex when we can sneak it, pass out and sleep past six a.m.

"So how'd the big family reunion go?" John wants to know. He gives himself a hug when he says this. I'm not sure what that's supposed to mean. Happy family, I guess.

"It was pretty uneventful," I say, and try not to tilt.

I realize I'm very drunk, drunker than I'd thought, drunker right now than is comfortable. I hope I'm not going to be sick. Careful not to look drunk, I bend down and pick up the bag of Goldfish. I grab a handful to settle my stomach. I pop the fish, one by one, into my mouth, one fish, two fish, Dr. Seuss fish, and try to think myself undrunk.

On TV, some horrible teenagers are together in a beach house. One is threatening another one with a pool cue. Another is on a bed, making shadow puppets on a wall as she talks loud on the phone. She makes a bunny. She makes a gator. "Oh no she didn't!" she's saying. The teenager with the pool cue yells, "Let's see what you got, bro."

"How can you watch this stuff?" I ask, and John shrugs and pops the last Oreo, which he kept hidden in his pocket, into his mouth.

"It was either this or *Ghost Hunters*," he says. "That ghost thing is for real, but I've seen all the episodes like three times. Last time, they got a picture of this ghost, face and all. It was hanging out on this staircase, just standing there, like it was waiting for something. Mind. Blown. I mean, if a picture's not proof, what is?"

If I weren't so drunk, I might tell John about the pictures my brother gave me, that kind of proof. I might say those pictures might as well be pictures of ghosts. I might say none of this seems completely real. I might ask John if he's considered the possibilities of Photoshop.

Instead I say, "Wow."

�||ॐ⋗

Once John leaves, I drop on the couch next to my husband, brush more crumbs onto the floor, and put my head on his lap. He flops a hand through my hair. I rub his thigh.

We're both exhausted. We smell like smoke. We smell like dirty hot dog water from the hot dogs boiling behind the counter at Jack's. My husband's pant leg is wet from someone's spilled beer, maybe mine.

"That went o.k., I think," I say.

He says, "They seem nice."

He says, "I like that they drink a lot."

He says, "It's interesting to see where you get your alcoholic tendencies from. And your paranoia, and some of that deep-seated crazy. You've done well for yourself, considering."

I say, "I thought it would be more dramatic somehow."

"It was dramatic," he says. "You didn't notice because of the pills and the booze."

"Maybe," I say, "but not like a movie."

"I didn't think they looked that much like you," he says.

"I thought they did," I say, and I make circles around my eyes, my face, meaning in some general way, I thought we looked alike.

"You know the kids are going to be up at fucking dawn," he says.

"Locklin, anyway," I say.

"So you think it was worth it?" he says, and I say, "Yeah, I do. I feel o.k. We all got along. It was fun."

What I don't say is that I'd hoped for more, maybe—a little less party, a little less booziness, fewer ghosts, a little less reality TV.

On TV, the teenagers are still at it. I reach for the remote right before the guy with the pool cue finally cracks somebody.

"Any chance for drunk sex or should I get a snack?" my husband says. I can feel his cock getting hard against my cheek. I move my hand there. I cup his balls and pull.

"Drunk sex, definitely," I say.

I say, "Just as soon as the crackers kick in. Just as soon as my stomach stops."

I think how good it would be to fuck him right now, to have that connection, my beautiful and patient blue-eyed husband, my best and most important family. I think about him turning me over and fucking me from behind. I think about turning around to look at him when he comes and so I look up at him now and his hair's crazy, in the way I love, the sides pressed flat and the top standing on end. He looks brilliant and insane. From this angle, I can see his eyelashes are drooping. They're so long they droop when he's tired. I keep one hand on his cock and rest the other on his chest so I can feel him breathing. I move my head up a little so I rise and fall with his breath. "I fucking love you," I say.

I'm pretty sure this is the last thing I say before I fall asleep.

34

In the morning, Locklin is up before six. He wants to go to the Monroeville Mall food court. He wants to go to Mister Rogers' Playground and climb the trolley and swing from some fake trees and poke X the Owl in the eyes.

"Go for the eyes," he says. It's something he learned when he was reading about sharks. It's something he'll teach his sister.

He's come into the bedroom and stands over us while we sleep. He does this a lot. I'm not sure how long he's standing there this morning before he reaches over and tries to wrench my husband's right eye open. Then he whacks my husband once in the forehead.

"Don't do that," my husband says, swatting.

Locklin whacks again and his dad swats back.

I open my eyes and try to focus. I realize my husband got me from the couch to the bed sometime earlier. He got me undressed and put a glass of juice next to me. I'm not sure if he ever got his snack. Now I'm half awake and Locklin scampers to my side of the bed. He tries to whack me, too, but I see it coming and roll.

"I'm done sleeping," he says.

"You weren't home last night to tuck me," he says. "I was thirsty."

He says, "I was calling for you."

He says, "John let me have the Oreos."

He says, "Where were you guys?"

He says, "I was worried."

John the babysitter hadn't said anything, but I can imagine the scene. Tucking Locklin in bed is a big deal. He uses two blankets. They have to be positioned just right—the first one stops at his waist, the second one meets it and goes up over his head. He sleeps like that, in a tricky cocoon, and if the blankets get messed up in the middle of the night—and they always get messed up in the middle of the night—he wakes, furious. Also, he needs warm cocoa to sleep. He needs two night-lights. He needs the hall lights on. He needs the kitchen light on. He needs to know where his parents are.

"Yeah, he's a piece of work that one," John says about Locklin, another reason we don't go out very often. It has to be for something important. Right now I'm not sure the night of bonding with my birth family had been all that important.

I squint and try to focus. My eyes are dry from the bar smoke, but I see Locklin coming in for round two. I turn my head right before he can land a finger jab.

"It's morning," he says. "Morning, morning, morning." Locklin dances in circles, giddy that his father and I, despite all our power, can't do anything about time.

I can't sleep and Locklin won't sleep so I get him set up in the living room with some Star Wars guys and a warm cocoa and a bowl shaped like an apple. I fill the bowl with Cheerios.

"There you go, buddy," I say, and pat him on his angry early-morning head.

The mall won't be open for hours, so X the Owl is out for now. If I can get Locklin settled, I can at least lie on the couch for a while. My head hurts. My stomach hurts. I thought family was supposed to feel different than a hangover.

"I don't want Cheerios. I don't want TV," Locklin says, sure he's being duped, which I guess he is. I put *The Empire Strikes Back* on anyway.

"It's for me, not you," I say, and hope it works.

Sometimes my son gets caught up in the connection between his toys and the screen. Sometimes he'll play like that for a long time, acting out scenes, adding his own dialogue and action. His first and favorite toy was a Woody doll from *Toy Story*. He made me write *Andy* on Woody's right boot. When people would ask Locklin what his name was, he'd say, "Andy." He'd say, "Howdy, partner."

He brought Woody to the hospital to visit my mother when she was sick. He propped Woody in the hospital bed next to her, then climbed in himself. They split her dinner tray. They fought over the Jello cup. The nurses made Locklin balloons from surgical gloves they'd blown up and tied off and he and my mother took turns whacking each other across the face with them. "It's slapstick," my mother said, "Get it?" as she whacked my son who whacked her back. They were rough with each other. They loved each other that much.

⚜

I knew my mother was dying when she was too tired to see Locklin. I knew she was dying when the thought of seeing her scared my son. When he talks about her now, he remembers the Jello cups. He remembers the times before she was sick, when they'd sit in the backyard and take turns howling like wolves at the moon.

"My old grandma," he says, "She lives in the sky."

"She can see you," he says.

Things I love about my son—his imagination, his love of story and small moments, the way he remembers the cadence of my mother's voice.

"You're in big trouble, missy," he says, and sounds just like her.

One of the things I wish about my son—that he'd let me fucking sleep.

⚜

"Hmph," he says now, about the movie, about this morning, about my failures as his mother. He crosses his small arms across his chest, but he plops on the floor in front of the TV anyway as the theme song kicks in.

The Empire Strikes Back is my favorite Star Wars movie.

I'm trying to convince Locklin it's the best one. It's a hard sell. He likes Jar Jar Binks. He likes the whiny, pre-adolescent Anakin, all the prequel stuff that, like a lot of kids' programming, makes me want to take my eyes out with an ice cream scoop. Right now my eyes would be easy to take out. They aren't just dry. They feel like they've been ashed in.

I lie down and hope Locklin lets me be. Phelan, I know, will sleep for hours. Even if she wakes up, she'll lie on her back in her crib and just tap the wall. Maybe she'll sing a bit—some *Baby Mozart* or Beethoven, hummed in perfect pitch—until one of us hears her and goes in. But with Locklin, I worry about closing my eyes, even as I'm closing them. I worry that everything within my son's reach—his bowl of cereal, the Star Wars figures, a red toy baseball bat—is a weapon.

⣔⣒

When I open my eyes again, the world feels off. Locklin is peaceful, curled up on the floor. He has his blanket pulled over his head. He looks like a caterpillar in a chrysalis. I can tell from his breathing that he's asleep. His toys are the wreckage after a storm, bodies strewn all around. I can hear my husband snoring in our bedroom. I can hear Phelan just starting to stir, her tiny pebble voice plinking down the hall.

Everything is so calm I hold still. I hold the moment and take it in and try not to break it.

On TV, Vader's just about to tell Luke he is his father.

203

35

The first message my birth mother sends comes through MySpace. The subject line reads "DO NOT RESPOND!" The message is "I will pray for you."

It's afternoon and my husband has taken both kids to the mall.

"Finally," Locklin had said.

Now the house is quiet, and I'm alone. I take another round of aspirin and settle in at the computer with coffee. I think I'll write an e-mail to my brother, thank him for the nice time, say how good it was to meet him. That's when I see the MySpace alert, a string of new messages in my inbox. When I see the first message, and then the line of messages after it, I start to shake. I shake and keep shaking. The messages are not nice. They are not good. They are the social media equivalent of Blonde4Eva's voicemails. *You bitch.*

I check the time the first message was written, 4 a.m. The other messages arrived minutes after that, one by one.

"I will pray for you," my birth mother repeats again and again.

There are other messages in my in-box, too, from

other people, strangers mostly. Someone sends an animated kitten dressed up as a soldier. Someone sends a glittering fairy. The kitten is firing an AK-47. The fairy flutters her legs and wishes me a magical day.

My birth mother does not wish me a magical day.

She wishes me dead.

This is what she says, "I've wished you dead. Many times."

"I want to forget you ever existed," she says. "I shut the door on you a long time ago."

"Go on with your life," she says. "Shame on you."

I try to get the coffee to my lips, but I spill it on the keyboard. I dab the keys with a Kleenex.

The messages go on shouting, all capital letters, battered exclamations.

My birth mother wants my attention.

She has it, and I have hers.

∽⊶⊷∾

I read the messages over and over. I feel a deep burn, nothing like love. Revulsion again, maybe.

The words my birth mother sends aren't anything I expected.

But what did I expect? What did I expect to feel? If not love, then a reckoning, maybe. Something healing, a kind of peace.

I think of the Catholic Charities counselor, how she laughed at my birth mother's rage. "She screamed and screamed at me," she said. "Imagine."

She said, "Sometimes things go wrong, but never like this."

It is ridiculous to expect anything healing from a woman who shouts a bone-shoed stranger down like that.

I am ridiculous.

My birth mother is right.

Shame on me.

"It's sad," I will tell my husband when he gets home, and I try to convince myself that it is, in fact, sad. She lives alone, and maybe she drinks and thinks too much and can't help herself.

"It is sad," my husband will say.

He will say, "I wish she wasn't so fucking mean."

He will say, "I think there's something really wrong with her."

He will say, "Are you o.k. with this?"

He will say, "I'm not o.k. with this."

For days, the messages keep coming. Every time my birth mother sends a new message, she deletes her profile, then puts another one in its place. There's never a photo, just a placeholder, the generic gray outline of a face, a question mark.

I think of John the babysitter, his *Ghost Hunters* show, how even a ghost has a face.

"Mind. Blown," John said.

I don't think my birth mother knows I have seen pictures of her. I'd like to tell her I know her posture is sharp, perfect, that she's prone to shoulder pads, that when she poses, she keeps her hands folded tight in her lap, controlled. I'd like to tell her the counselor at Catholic Charities sits the same way.

I'd like to tell her they're both trying to keep secrets that aren't secrets any more.

I'd like to tell her I know she looks nothing like me. I'd like to tell her this makes me happy, that we look nothing alike, but she keeps deleting herself so I can't respond, which doesn't seem fair, which seems exactly the way it's always been between us.

If I can't see her face, I can't tell her how ugly she is.

If I can't touch her shoulders, I can't walk her away from my life.

I've never had a voice in any of this.

⤞⟨⟩⤝

Years ago, a friend gave me a book by Nancy Verrier called *The Primal Wound*. "I think you need this," she said. "It might explain why you're such an asshole sometimes."

Verrier says adult adopted people think what they do and say has no impact on the people around them. This is because, as infants, adoptees scream and scream for mothers who never come.

Verrier says this is how adoptees learn our voices have no power.

This is how we learn we don't matter much at all.

⤞⟨⟩⤝

From the messages she sends, I know my birth mother knows my brother and I have met. She knows my sister and I have met, and my birth mother won't forgive her for it.

My birth mother says I should get my own family. She tells me on MySpace who my father is. She tells me I should go bother him. She says there's no denying because I look so much like him. She calls him the Jew. She calls me the Jew too, like this is something filthy to her.

My birth mother says doesn't want to meet me, not at a basketball game, not ever.

"There will be no gaming," she writes.

I don't go to basketball games. My birth mother wouldn't know that.

I don't get to ask why she's saying any of this.

I don't get to tell her I don't want to meet her, either.

⸎

Anger begets anger.

I'd like to tell her how pathetic her idea of a meeting is—a basketball game, where she'd be standing with her hot dog, her plastic cup of warm beer, her floppy t-shirt. I'd walk up, dressed in my one good black suit, but she wouldn't know it was my only one, she wouldn't know I couldn't afford a second suit. I'd tell her how little she resembled the woman I thought she'd be. I'd compliment her on her excellent taste in sneakers. I'd ask her if she bought them in Paris. I'd ask her if she's ever read Hemingway. I'd ask her where she went to college. I'd be a bitch, the

209

bitch to end all bitches. I'd poke a hole in my throat and smoke a cigarette there, and then I'd heal myself. I'd offer to buy her a beer, another Budweiser, what Germans call *American jauche*, Yankee piss, but I'm sure she knows that, since she fucked my father, a German and a Jew, who was lucky to get away, because she probably wished him dead, the way she did me.

We were both, my father and I, lucky. We made it over the wall.

If my birth mother wants to invoke prayers, this is my prayer to her, all terribleness and scorn, but I can't say it. I'm still a baby in a crib, screaming in an empty room, learning my voice is nothing, not even air.

⟳

"It's not you," my brother says when I tell him about all of this. "It's her. She does it to me, too. She drinks. She gets mean. We're used to it. Just don't read the messages."

But I do read them, or I ask my husband to read them and translate for me. He does this, and keeps the cruelest parts out.

I think I'm like those teenage girls who take pictures of themselves duck-facing in the mirror, then hang around online and wait for someone to tell them they're pretty.

I don't need my birth mother to say something kind to me.

I go on waiting for my birth mother to say something kind to me.

The messages keep coming and there's nothing kind
about them. "She's paranoid," my brother says. "She
drinks and it gets worse. I told you it runs in the family.
Don't let it bother you."

Already I love my brother. That I met him is its own
miracle.

"Maybe this will help," my sister had said, as if the
truth—about me, my birth, my life—was a buoy that had
surfaced just in time.

But I don't know what my birth mother needs and I
don't want to help her. I don't want to help her any more
than she wants to help me.

⊶⧽⧽⊷

Of course I would help her.

She's my mother.

⊶⧽⧽⊷

I want what my birth mother wished for herself. I want to
forget she ever existed. I want to sever what's left of the
blood connection between us. I think of her as a bad vein,
ugly, varicose, the kind of vein doctors have to burn and
seal to stop the blood flow.

I'd like another shot at the Catholic Charities questionnaire.

"And what is your expected outcome?"

211

I'd scratch out "medical history."
I'd write in, "cauterization."
I'd have to explain that.

⤜⧉⤛

"While you are pursuing your fantasy as to how you were so left behind!!" my birth mother writes. "Shame on you! Your ancestors were hard working and proud individuals and you just beat that down!"

I don't know what I've beaten down. What she calls my fantasy, my adoption, isn't a fantasy. It's fact. There's something to the word, though, so I look it up, which is what I do with words a lot lately, trying to understand things.

Fantasy has many roots—Middle English, Old French, Latin, and finally Greek, from phantom, *phantazein*. It means "to make visible."

⤜⧉⤛

I am my birth mother's secret and so I should stay invisible, the opposite of fantasy.

My birth mother's e-mails seem like fantasies. They imply conversations, a dialogue, as if we've been talking for years. She sets up her MySpace profiles under the names of rock stars.

The latest profile she uses is Joan Jet. One T.

"If she's going to do that," I tell my husband, "she should at least get the spelling right."

212

For a blip in college, I dressed like Joan Jett, black jean jacket and tight jeans, spiked mullet, tough stance, one elbow on the bar. I tossed back shots and pretended I didn't throw up in dive bar bathrooms and rest my head on the filthy toilets afterward and get carried out, my hair wet with piss and puke. I held cigarettes I never smoked. I pointed at people with my chin. I pretended not to care about anyone until I almost became the fantasy I imagined for myself.

"We get that from Mommy," my brother said.

One time, Joan Jett played a free concert on the pier in Erie, PA. I got there early to get a spot next to the stage. The crowd pushed forward when Joan came on, beautiful as a brushstroke. She played "Bad Reputation" and stomped the stage in high-top sneakers. I was dressing like Madonna by then, all lace and ribbons and black silk gloves, but it was Joan I loved first. I reached up as high as I could, but there were so many people, so many hands. Then a stranger, this thick biker-looking guy in a jean jacket with the sleeves ripped off, hoisted me up. He carried me on his shoulders, swaying like a flag, until I got Joan's attention and she came to the end of the stage and bent down. I expected her to high five maybe, one hard slap, but instead she held my hand. It was only for a second maybe.

Then she let go, backed away and punched the air with a fist.

❧

"I mean, what's wrong with her?" I ask my husband about my birth mother.

"She's crazy," my husband says. "You don't have to do this. I'll handle her. I'll stop it. Do you want me to send her a message? She's old-school. She's a bully, but she'll listen to a man. She'll fuck with you, but she won't fuck with me. One e-mail from me and this will stop. She'll think I'm her Irish father coming after her with a belt, or something pathetic. Women like that, at that age, are scared of men. Tell me when you've had enough."

I've had enough, but there are still things I need to know. My birth mother knows them, so I don't say stop. I sit and shake and wait to see how much longer.

"There's the medical history," I say.

My husband says, "Fuck that. Medical histories aren't roadmaps. You can live without it, and our kids can live without it. You brother can tell us whatever we need to know. Like it's good you don't smoke cigarettes, since your birth mother currently inhales Winston Lights through a hole in her throat."

❧

I imagine her, 68 years old, alone in the dark. The light from the computer screen turns her face blue. The gray

214

silhouette, the question mark, reflects in her glasses. The shadows of everything come back. I feel her fingers on the keys, the anger rising up. Her face looks underwater. She's trying to push down the past. The past, like a drowning victim, refuses to stay down.

"What's done is done," she writes.

And I think no, it's not.

36

My next e-mail is from Blonde4Eva. It's a chain letter. She's supposed to send it to her ten closest friends. There are five people in the address line. I'm number two. The letter starts:

True Friendship
None of that Sissy &*^% !

It goes on and on until it reaches this list:

1.   When you are sad—I will help you get drunk and plot revenge against the sorry bastard who made you sad.

2.   When you are blue—I will try to dislodge whatever is choking you.

3.   When you smile—I will know you finally got laid.

4.   When you are scared—I will rag on you about it every chance I get.

When you are worried—I will tell you horrible stories about how much worse it could be until you quit whining.

5.   When you are confused—I will use little words.

6.   When you are sick—Stay the hell away from me until you are well again I don't want whatever you have.

7.   When you fall—I will point and laugh at your clumsy ass.

8.   This is my oath..... I pledge it to the end. "Why?" you may ask; "because you are my friend."

Send this to 10 of your closest friends, then get depressed because you can only think of 4.

Friendship is like peeing your pants, everyone can see it, but only you can feel the true warmth.

⋞⋟

The subject of the next e-mail from Blonde4Eva reads "You Bitch."

It's written all in caps and highlighted in neon green.

⋞⋟

The next e-mail from my birth mother reads, "There are things that should be left alone and this is one of them."

218

When my birth mother calls me the mistake, she writes the word in all caps, just in case I don't understand.

37

I become my own mistake. I lose weeks.

My days start to move in casino time, Target retail time, drunk-in-a-bar time—something has happened to the light, someone's messed with the clocks, the wrong sounds are too loud, and the right sounds—the voices of people I love—turn to static.

I can hear my family—the splash and whir of the dishwasher, Locklin playing with his Star Wars figures, his laser battle sounds, my husband typing away on a new book manuscript, Phelan banging the floor in time to the *Barney* theme song. I hear all of this and know I should get up. I should go and be with my family. I should make dinner. It's almost dinnertime.

Instead I sit and stare at the computer. I'm a mime in a box. I'm an expired coupon, an empty slot machine with its bells smashed out. I'm waiting, pathetic as it is, for that one line of kindness, one line of love, more hate. I'm waiting for one final line of cruelty to sever everything.

I do not call this what it is: grieving.

What I know: this will not end well.

I think of my parents' tombstone, the words carved

there. Rest in peace. Together forever. United as one. Amen. Amen.

The mother I've never met says I'm a monster.

38

For years, my dad, the father who raised me, gambled. He placed bets, he waited, and he lost. He played numbers. He played the lottery. He kept his losing lottery tickets. He played my mother's birthday, my birthday, as if love would make him lucky. He thought and schemed, mashed numbers and ideas, and never won.

"You come from a long line of writers," my friend Tony Buba, who grew up in Braddock with my dad and my uncles, told me once. I was confused. Tony is a filmmaker, big on visuals. He held out his hand and pretended to scribble. He said, "You didn't think that deli your uncle ran was really about chipped ham, did you?" He said, "Numbers, sweetheart." He said, "Those guys wrote a lot of numbers."

A numbers-writer is called a bookie. In Pittsburgh in the 70s and 80s, everyone had a bookie, same as everyone had a family doctor. I didn't know, growing up, that a bookie was illegal.

Now I write books. Growing up, I didn't know writing could be a dangerous thing.

A decade after my dad's death, my cousin John, his nephew, will hit the lottery and win a million dollars. He'll have to split it three ways—one co-worker, one girlfriend—but still. John will say, "See, I always knew we came from a family of winners."

My father didn't live to hear this. I lived to hear this, but I don't believe it. I am my father, the man who raised me but was not my blood. I gamble to lose.

Because of the terrible things that happened to my father, he called people cockroaches. I think of my birth mother like that, a hard shell, refusing to die, scaring everyone she crawls past.

39

"Mom?" Locklin says. He's come downstairs. I didn't hear his footsteps. I don't look up. I slouch over the computer and stare at the screen. "Mom, mom, mom, mom, mom?"

"Shh. Mommy's working," I say. "Mommy's busy."

I hate myself.

My birth mother wants this and so I give it to her, my self-loathing my penance, a gift.

My mother, my real mother, would not like me neglecting my family like this. When she was alive, she was always thinking of us, of Locklin especially. She'd leave bags of diapers and bulk toilet paper tucked behind our screen door—"There was a sale, buy-one-get-one." She'd pick up toys at garage sales and leave them in the driveway covered in big bows. She'd call and ask to babysit so I could go to the grocery alone. She'd make pies and cream puffs and pull up unexpected in her little red car, wearing fake Ray-Bans and Keds, and say, "I thought you could use a treat."

Even when she knew she was very sick, my mother would try to do things to help. She said it kept her mind off her own problems. She said the best thing was to keep her hands busy and make herself useful. She would not see what I am doing now as useful. I can feel her disgust the way I can feel my son standing behind me as I tap away at the computer keys.

What I type to my birth mother, to Blonde4Eva: *Fuck you.* Delete. *You misunderstand everything.* Delete. *No. Seriously. Fuck You.* Delete. *How dare you. You're the bitch.* Delete. *You're the mistake mistake mistake.*

I can feel my son shift from right foot to left and back. I know he's pacing in place. I know he does this when he's sad and nervous and anxious. I know this and I know he's doing it now and I do not turn around.

❧

The other day Locklin arranged his Lego guys on my computer keys. All of them were in combat poses—lightsabers against swords, guns against bullwhips, knives against tiny plastic fists. There were so many Lego guys it looked like a war. No one was winning.

If I thought about it, I'd have realized my son was trying to talk to me in my own language. He was trying to show me something, a metaphor. My son, tired of fighting for my attention, showed me a battle, but I wouldn't see it. Instead, I was annoyed. One of Luke Skywalker's little Lego feet jammed my backspace key and I had to pry it loose.

"Goddamn it, Locklin," I said.

I am a terrible mother.

Like the birth mother before me, and so on and so on.

And this time my mother, my real mother, a good mother, is not here to tell me otherwise.

I think if she were here, this time she'd agree.

40

"You're family," my brother says. "Family," my sister says. They stretch the syllables of the word out.

They have a large family—lots of cousins. They have huge reunions, with booze and burgers and traditions where people wear hats with shamrock antennae and jingle-bell sweaters and call each other names like asshat and pussynuts and hug like they won't let go.

Family. The word is a mantra, a totem, a skyline that goes on forever until it drops off at the end of the world.

I think my brother and sister believe if they say the word enough, it will become true for me, too, like maybe it will be o.k. for me to just show up at the next family picnic and no one will ask questions about the stranger at the buffet table, loading her pockets with cocktail shrimp and beanie-weenies.

"Enjoy your family," my birth mother writes. "You with your sick curiosity," and of course she writes the words family and sick in all caps.

"You should just block her," my brother tells me, but I keep thinking she'll crack.

I need to believe in my birth mother's buried softness

the way I need to know I and my children haven't inherited a terrible disease.

⊷⊱⊰⊶

If paranoia and cruelty run like cancer in my birth mother's bloodline, I'm hoping something else will show up to provide balance and grace.

I re-read the Catholic Charities report, looking for anything I might have missed. That's where I find it—not in e-mails or late-night phone calls, but in an otherwise unremarkable account of my birth mother's last visit to the orphanage. It's written in formal social-work speak, bloodless, but now it feels urgent, a lost credit card in a pocket, a slivered fingernail at a crime scene.

It's evidence and a way to move on.

41

Catholic Charities Non-Identifying Report: Last Contact
The birth mother visits the orphanage at Rosalia

Marie comes to the crib, but will not hold the child. She will not call the child by name. It has been nearly a year. Marie wears her good green suit. She wears her eyeglasses. Her hair is curled, sprayed, pinned, everything proper as a doily. Marie is thin again, thinner even. She looks, she thinks, like a librarian, quiet, not one to make a fuss.

"Do not bring more shame to yourself," Eveleen said when she advised Marie not to do this, but Marie didn't see how there was any more shame left to bring.

Still, here at the crib, she does not make a fuss. The child is sleeping and Marie hopes not to wake it when she lifts the child's shirt and touches its belly. The skin is soft, warm, like the inside of Marie's wrist. Marie does not turn the covers down to look at the mangled legs, the brace already pulling them straight. Marie tries to not look at the face. She tries to focus only on the belly. She leaves her hand there. She asks if the child seems happy.

The social worker says yes. Marie asks if the child will be cared for. The social worker says yes. Marie looks only at the belly and thinks of a white balloon, something to tuck a message inside and let go.

Marie asks if the child will have the necessary surgeries. The social worker says yes. Marie makes the social worker repeat this. The social worker does.

Then Marie takes her hand away.

A let-go balloon is something for strangers to find.

42

After my son and daughter were born, a nurse bandaged their umbilical wounds. I had to clean the wounds with alcohol, a tiny cotton swab. The wounds oozed. They looked poisonous, like mushrooms, bulbous pulsing things. I had to be careful to keep them clean until they healed, scabbed over, then finally fell off and I'd find them on the carpet, mistaking them at first for shriveled hot dog bits. It was primitive and, mostly, gross. It was not the stuff of baby books.

But those wounds marked the place where we were connected once—the clearest marker between us—so maybe I should have felt something other than revulsion, other than the desire for those horrible stumps to hurry up, heal, and disappear.

Maybe it was important for my birth mother to touch me in the exact spot where we had been connected. Maybe it was very painful for her to do that, or maybe it was less painful, a distance thing. Maybe the spot marks severing, not connection.

Maybe she couldn't bear to touch me anywhere else.

43

I choose to believe in my birth mother's underground tenderness and mercy. I choose to believe the Catholic Charities report is proof, and so I write her a long e-mail. One night, before she has a chance to delete herself, I send it to her.

I tell her about my parents. I tell her they gave me a good life. I tell her my father made sure I went to college, and then later to graduate school. I tell her he believed I was born smart, and maybe that came from her. I tell her I've traveled to Paris and Rome, beyond that. I've lived in New York. I tell her I've had a good life. I think this will matter to her because it would matter to me if I were her. I tell her I've tried not to waste the life she started for me. I've seen the ruins at Ephesus. I've been to the Coliseum. I understand a little about history. I understand a little about family and the risks people take to build one. I have my own now. I tell her I am trying to focus on what that means. I tell her my daughter looks exactly like I did when I was a baby. I tell her my son has my eyes and my hands. I tell her my daughter has my husband's sweet personality. I tell her my son is more like me, that he worries.

I tell her I'm sure this doesn't matter to her but it matters to me to say it.

I tell her again—I have had a good life and I am grateful for it.

I use that word—grateful.

I write it down and settle it between us the way I settled it with my mother, my real mother, before she died. I sat next to her on her bed, her head in my lap, and stroked her hair and felt it fall out between my fingers.

"I'm tired," she said.

"I know," I said.

"I'm glad you're settled," she said. "I'm glad you have a family."

She said, "I thought for a long time it would never happen."

She said, "I'm sorry I wasn't a better mother."

"But you were," I said. "You were a great mother."

"No," she said. "I was nervous all the time."

"You were a good mother," I said.

"You're a good mother," she said.

I thanked her.

She said, "You're welcome."

"No," I said, "I mean for all of it. I mean for my life."

"Oh that," my mother, my real mother, the mother who raised me, said.

⌖

In the end I was so grateful. I wanted my mother finally to know it.

Now I tell my birth mother I'm grateful, too. I tell her I can't imagine how hard this must have been on her. I tell her what my mother, my real mother, the mother who raised me, used to say, "Not flesh of my flesh, but heart of my heart." I tell my birth mother she did the very best thing by giving me up to this woman who loved me and who I loved.

My birth mother responds the next day with a short e-mail that says: "I've thought of you often. It's just too much after all these years. What's done is done."

⊸⸱⸱⊶

And then, later, she sends another e-mail that says she wishes she'd aborted me.

She says she would have, had she known.

44

೪

Our friend Ed is over for dinner when I notice something odd about Phelan. We're at the dining room table. I've made paella and poured wine. I've talked about my birth-mother, her emails, how she wanted me aborted. Ed is offering advice. Ed is a poet and one of the most reason-able people I know and lately our house has been short on reason.

"It seems to me pretty silly to give yourself over to that kind of cruelty," he says, and now with a little distance I think, of course it is.

The e-mails have stopped. My husband did what he promised—I said I'd had enough and he sent an e-mail to my birth mother after her abortion comment. He asked her to stop contacting me. He told her I wanted nothing more to do with her. He said wonderful things about me as his wife and as a mother. He told her that her messages were not welcome in his house. She sent one e-mail back, formal as a passport, saying she would stop and she did. Blonde4Eva stopped, too.

And so, even short on reason, I'm better. Having Ed here helps. In graduate school, when I wanted to wear leather jackets and be famous, Ed reminded me that books were my life's work, that the other things I wanted—the stupid, superficial stuff—only happened with reading and writing and making my own book, and by then I wouldn't want the superficial stuff anyway. So much of what I have and how I live comes from the few years I spent with Ed in my early twenties—the magazines I used to publish in, the writers conferences I attended, the connections I made, the first books I fell in love with. Now Ed is at my table, drinking wine, being his good calm self.

The house feels peaceful. Locklin plays by himself in the living room. Phelan watches *Baby Mozart* tapes and hums along. I leave her out of her brace, and she's happy to be free. She tries dancing and looks like a pink accordion bouncing up and down on her chubby knees. Then she toddles over to the table, where the subject has shifted to poetry, and reaches for a hug. I bend down to my daughter and pull her close. That's when I notice it. There's a smell coming from her face, around her mouth, her nose. I look closer and she tilts her head back for a kiss. The smell gets stronger, like moldy potatoes.

"Remember when she wouldn't kiss you?" my husband says. He starts to tell Ed the story about the way Phelan used to back away from me. She'd kiss her brother. She'd kiss her father. She wanted nothing to do with me. She'd run from me into my husband's arms.

"No, there's something wrong," I say.

I look at Ed, I look at my husband. I look up Phelan's left nostril, then her right. I can't see, but there's pus crusted around the right nostril. I pull her onto my lap and turn her upside down and she starts crying.

"I think there's something stuck up there," I say.

I lean forward and the smell is undeniable, rancid, rotting. It's clear she's jammed something in her nose, though I can't see what. It's wedged in and, from the smell, it's been there a while, which is dangerous. My husband tells me to calm down, Ed makes a joke, but I know my daughter. She has a history of this, stuffing things up her nose—bits of diaper, tissue, Styrofoam. We've been to the hospital more than once and my husband and I had to hold her down while she thrashed and screamed as the doctor pried fluff out of her, like she was one of her own stuffed bears.

"Some kids like to do this," the doctor explained. "It makes them feel secure."

Usually, though, I noticed right away or caught Phelan mid-stuff. When had this latest incident happened? What makes a beautiful girl-child stuff her nose with anything? Was she feeling insecure? More insecure than usual? I think about infections, complications, the nose so close to the brain. I press my lips to Phelan's forehead, which feels hot. Her hands feel hot, too. I think of the infection already moving through her.

How could I miss this? How could I be so consumed by my own life that I'd missed hers? That night we'd gone out to meet my brother and sister and left the kids with the sitter. Maybe this happened then. Or maybe it happened right in front of me and I didn't look up, didn't notice anything at all.

Which would be worse?

ﻌﻗﻟﻌ

Ed leaves and we pack up and take Phelan to Children's Hospital, where we wait in a room with a giant poster of cartoon faces. The poster is meant to show children in stages of distress. There's a 1 to 10 scale. A 1 is a smiley face. It means a child is pain-free. A 10—a child in full-on distress—is a face scrunched into an asterisk. It means the child needs to be sedated. The poster's titled "Understanding Your Child's Pain."

Locklin points to each face, asks his sister, "Is it like this, Phe? Or this?" Phelan settles down. She thinks it's a game. She nods like every face on the wall is a match, like she feels everything all at once. Somewhere in other rooms, other people's children cry. The sounds echo and bounce off then through my skin.

My daughter is in my husband's arms. He's so good with her.

ﻌﻗﻟﻌ

My husband and Locklin stay in the waiting room. I carry Phelan back into an exam room, where the doctors buckle her into a full-body brace. It looks like something from *Silence of the Lambs*. It looks like something from a carnival, a magic act, like someone's about to throw knives. Her tiny arms are strapped down. Her legs are strapped down. Her head is anchored and strapped into

242

place. The whole time she screams. I cry. I try not to cry and I cry. The doctors ask me to stay back. They rotate my daughter backwards. She screams but can't move her head. From the angle they have her at, she can't see me. She has no way of knowing I'm still here. I keep telling her I am, but I'm not sure she can hear me over her own screams. I worry she thinks she's alone. I worry she thinks I've left her. The doctors tell me again to please stay back so I do. I try to be good, cooperative. I try not to make a fuss. My daughter is screaming. I raise my voice. I try to keep talking so she can hear me, so I can hear myself.

"I'm here, Phe," I say. "It's o.k. I'm here."

I say, "I'm right here."

I say, "I'm not going anywhere."

I say, "It will be over in a minute."

I say, "I've got you, Phe."

I say, "Mommy's here."

When they tilt her back down, tears have flooded her face. Her eyes are wide, a small animal's caught on a highway. She doesn't see me at first and then she does.

The doctors loosen the straps and I rush over to hold my daughter.

She grabs on and cries so hard I think she'll come apart.

≈⊙⎮⎮⊙≈

When it's over, I sit in a plastic chair and rock Phelan. She's calming down. My son and husband are still in the other room. The doctor's gone out to get them. There's

243

the sound of metal instruments being cleaned and other children weeping. There's the sound of my own thoughts.

Even now I imagine my birth mother, comforting, calming her own children, the ones she doesn't wish she'd aborted, the ones she raised, though she could be a woman who never comforted anyone, who believed comfort was weakness, that caring lacked strength. I try to picture it, one scene, one moment, and then I can't and it doesn't matter.

I pull my daughter closer. I hear my thoughts, and then I stop hearing them. There are so many voices, voices over voices, better ones to hear.

❧

Later one of the doctors, a pretty young woman in a ponytail, holds out a vial so I can see. Inside is what she's plucked from deep in my daughter's nose. There's some of the usual white fluff and one hard red ball. I look for a minute before I recognize it. Phelan's plucked the plastic nose off her Rudolph the Red-Nosed Reindeer and stuffed it up her own.

"She stuffed a nose up her nose," the doctor says, laughing. "That's a new one."

Phelan, hearing the pretty doctor laugh, does her best to laugh too, but it comes out choked and it's hard to breathe so she starts crying again.

❧

Time will soften this moment, the way it does most things. My daughter will grow and keep growing into her own beautiful, still happy self, and this will become a family story, a joke we'll share over and over.

"A nose up her nose," I'll say.

My husband will say, "It's better than when she shredded her diaper and stuffed that up her nose."

At Christmas, my son will tease, "You could even say she glowed."

The story will become one of our favorites. I won't be great at keeping up with baby books and scrapbooks, but I will remember all the stories and my husband will remember all the stories and we will tell our children these stories on demand.

We will tell them on holidays and at the dinner table and at bedtime. We will tell them when we drink. We will tell them to our friends. We will tell them the way old ladies in church tick off prayers on rosary beads, which is how I think of family now, the most sacred thing.

45

This is from a long time ago but I want to tell it like it's happening now. I want to say now, in the present, because it feels that way.

I think it always will.

❦

My father wants to go to the food court at Monroeville Mall. It's a month, maybe, before he'll die. He wants Chick-fil-a. This is before my mother is sick. This is before the insurance company delivers the hospital bed and oxygen tanks and walker to my parents' home and my father asks the delivery guy how long people live after he delivers things like that.

"On average," my father says to the guy, who's a kid really, a kid who wants to drop and run.

My father says, "I mean, a week, two tops?" He's angry and wants to fight.

My father says, "So how long do I have, doctor?"

The kid looks down at his feet, which are covered in blue paper booties so he doesn't track dirt in the house.

The booties look like the ones surgeons wear, which isn't helping. The kid shifts his weight right, left. "I just bring what's on the form, sir," he says.

I don't know how many people ask him things like this. Not many, I hope. Not many people are like my father. I imagine most people sit back and stare, like this kid's wheeling in their coffins. Maybe they say thank you. Maybe they tell him to have a nice day.

Me, I'm on leave from my job. I work for the airlines, where I don't have to deal with any one person for long. I'm a flight attendant. Everything is temporary. Welcome aboard, would you like a beverage, fasten your seat belts, tray tables up, cell phones off, thank you, goodbye. In ways the job is a good fit, transient, drop and run, like me.

But now I'm home to help my mother take care of my father, who is furious because he's dying. His cancer was in remission. Now it's not.

I say now because sometimes a clock ticking is just sound and writing in the present lets my parents be alive, which is what I want them to be.

Up until this moment, my father thought he'd been saved. He told the waitress at Red Lobster he'd been saved. He told the organist at church. He told the mailman and the UPS guy. He'd been praying. He carried a blue prayer book in his chest pocket. He thought it was working. It was the happiest and most hopeful I've ever see him.

At Red Lobster, he ordered dessert, a chocolate volcano cake. "I have a lot to celebrate," he told the waitress. "This bastard doctor said I was going to die and I prayed and prayed and God answered, so now I'm not dying."

But the prayer book and God both quit. It must have been something he'd done, my father figured. Something he hadn't counted on.

To the delivery kid, my father says, "The world will bite you in the ass, you watch."

My father says, "You mark my words."

He says, "How much they pay you to do a thing like this?"

≺◦⎰⎱◦≻

It's hot in the food court. The mall's dry heat cranks up. It's late January, but not snowing. My father wears his heavy knit cap, the one from when he was in the Navy. He was in World War II, on an aircraft carrier. He knew people who died. People he didn't know died around him. One man, in a bunk near my father's, died when a kamikaze hit the side of the ship. They'd both been sleeping. The man never saw land, never traveled home, never saw Japan as anything other than a target.

When my father landed in Hiroshima after the bomb, he gave a woman there his cigarettes and his shoes. He gave a man his Timex watch. These are the kinds of details my father gives. Cigarettes, shoes, a watch that kept good time, a bunk mate with shit luck. Nothing about what he saw, not really. Nothing about what he felt. Nothing about what he feels.

Nothing about how close his bunkmate's sleeping body may have been to his own.

It has never occurred to me how little I know about my father. I can list the things he seems to care about. It isn't a long list. I know he liked to sing and then gave up singing. I know he drove an Iron City beer truck before he was legal to drive. I know his father once beat him for ruining a pair of shoes in a puddle. I know his father beat him a lot. My father believes in God and the Pennsylvania lottery. I know when they were young, my father and a neighborhood kid got in a fight in an alley in Braddock. It was something about shoes in a puddle. I know my father won and was proud and believed it meant something. I know he went on believing it meant something even when the kid became a millionaire owner of a Pittsburgh pizza joint and my father retired from the mills and had to sell the house in Florida he'd spent his savings on because his wife ended up with a bad heart and couldn't take the heat.

The world is cruel but my father always remembers he once kicked a famous pizza guy's ass. At any minute, things could have gone another way. I think that has always been my father's logic. I think that's how he's survived.

"They have a C rating from the Health Department," my mother says about the famous guy's pizza place, out of loyalty to my father.

My father says, "Cockroaches won't eat pizza from that son of a bitch."

❧❧

After my father dies, I'll find a box of his war medals. I'll find yellowed baggies filled with Japanese yen, the Emperor's face on the bills. I'll find a picture of my father in his sailor uniform, his arm around another sailor whose name I'll never know. Maybe this was his dead bunkmate. Maybe this man was a friend. I've never known my father to have many friends.

I'll find my father's uniform and, years after that, my son will try it on. Locklin will be 12 years old when he does this. He won't be able to fit his arms through the sleeves.

I'll tell him my father lied about his age to go to war. I'll say I don't know why.

My son will say, "I think they made people smaller back then."

∽∘{}∘∾

I try to get my father situated at a table in the middle of the food court. It's hard for him to be comfortable. The chairs are hardwood. Everything hurts. He's wearing a sweatsuit my mother got him a few weeks back. It fit then. Now he looks like a child who's raided his father's closet.

Under the knit cap, his face is gray. His cheekbones look sharp enough to poke through his skin. I don't remember ever noticing his cheekbones before. His face has always been round, doughy. He's always looked eerily like a cross between Carroll O'Connor, who played Archie Bunker on *All in the Family*, and John Paul II, the Polish Pope.

"You have Archie's miserable personality and the Pope's good looks," my mother likes to joke. "You should get yourself one of those Pope Mobiles. You should have a parade."

"Watch yourself," my father says, and crosses himself to be sure. "The Pope is no joke."

My Polish father grew up holy—Easter wafers and vials of holy water in his house, pictures of Jesus everywhere, medallions with pictures of saints around his neck.

My father has always believed in something.

Now I'm not sure what's left.

⌘

The food court light is harsh, fluorescent. If I didn't know this man was my father, I wouldn't recognize him.

"You'd think the bastards could afford decent chairs," he says, and shifts from side to side like he's trying to find a position that's tolerable. His hips jut out, so he sits on bone.

He's that thin, I think, though I won't see for myself until weeks from now, when I have to bathe and change him. Then I will see my father's naked body for the first time. The sight of him—uncircumcised, nearly hairless, his nipples and chest small as a boy's, the dark urine filling the catheter bag, foam filling his mouth when he breathes and I have to keep suctioning it out and suctioning it out even though the hospice nurse tells me I shouldn't, that it's natural, normal, that I should let it go, it's natural, all of this is natural—will almost be too much.

⊷⊶

Right now, though, my father is alive. He is hungry for grease and chicken, even if he knows the food will not sit right. He wants his sandwich and some waffle fries and a Coke. He wants to sit and watch people, even though he doesn't like people much. He's always liked to do this. He likes to come to the mall and sit and and think about how most of the people he watches are probably pretty terrible when it comes down to it.

I like to people-watch, too. It's one of the things my father and I have in common. For now I think people are more interesting than terrible. As long as we don't talk much, my father and I can sometimes sit together like this and get along.

Usually, though, my father can't help himself.

"Look at that bastard," he will say, pointing out this person or that for no reason I can see. "Look at that jag-off."

My father always looks for evidence that the world is a terrible place.

He finds it everywhere.

⊷⊶

I loved my father more than anything when I was young. "Daddy," I will tell my daughter. "Daddy was my first word." My second word was "hi," and my third word was "circus," because my father took me to the circus at the Civic Arena in Pittsburgh in 1966. He wanted, maybe, to show me a different world, one more amazing and beautiful and controlled than the one I'd been born into. In this other world, people bought tickets and got what they paid for—a glittering elephant that bowed to a poodle, a clown that spit fire and didn't get burned, a tiger that jumped through a hula hoop, a lion that stood on its hind legs clawing at nothing, like even the air was a cage.

"You were so excited you pissed all over me, princess," my father likes to say when he tells this story. "You soaked me straight down to my underwear."

He laughs every time he says this. My father doesn't laugh much.

∽⧉∾

I go get a newspaper and bring it back. "Will you be o.k.?" I say, and spread the paper out in front of him. My father pushes it away and says, "What the hell do you think? I'm not going anywhere. Where the hell do you think I'd go?"

He looks away from me, across the food court, where a goth kid is slouched over a slice of pizza, and says, "Look at that jackass."

By the time I gather up our drinks and food tray and head back to the table, my father looks tired. He glances at the tray and says, "Ketchup. You forgot the ketchup. How could you forget ketchup?"

I go get ketchup, extra napkins, salt, anything else I can think of so there's nothing left to set him off. I cup everything in my hands and set it on the table between us like an offering.

"Huh," he says, and scowls.

For decades, I've tried not to be like my father. "You're just like him," my mother says when she wants to get to me. "I'm adopted," I say, to explain away the differences.

One of my greatest fears has always been that my mother would die first and I'd be left alone to take care of my father.

Now I'm sure that won't happen.

⚜

My father stares at the tray, like he's confused. I unwrap both sandwiches and put one in front of him and one in front of me. I spread the fries on the tray and salt them up. I put the straws in our drinks. I divide the napkins, a pile for him, a pile for me. I squirt ketchup into a mound on one napkin and place it close to my father so he doesn't have to reach. He still doesn't move.

"You o.k.?" I say.

"Stop asking me that," he says.

All around us, the sounds of the food court seem louder. A lady from the Chinese food place pushes tooth-picked chicken at people. "Szechuan lunch special sample, try today," she says. She thrusts her tray, stopping traffic. The hot dog vendors yell, "How are you today?" to no one. The fan from the cookie shop is angled so the brownie smell mixes with the hot dog grill and the Chinese place and the burnt dough from the pizza place and it's not good, any of it. If the food doesn't make my father nauseous, I think the smells will. There are voices everywhere, families with small children, mothers saying, "No you may not x, and no you may not y," groups of women and old men gossiping. Cherry incense floats down from Spencer's Gifts. The soundtrack is a Muzak version of what I finally figure out is Fleetwood Mac's "Tusk."

"Remember when I did the baton routine to this in high school?" I say to my father, pointing into the air, to where the Musak fills things up, as if he'll know that song and get what I'm saying. "I knocked myself out with my baton trying to do a two-turn. They had to call in the school nurse. I had a lump in my eyebrow for a week. All those lessons you paid for never helped. I was awful."

He still hasn't moved to eat.

He looks up at me and I think he wants to talk about those lessons, what a waste, or about something else I've forgotten or done that is ruining this meal for him.

Instead he says, "He touched me."

"What?" I say.

The cancer, I know, has gone to my father's brain. It's affecting his vision and other things, too. Sometimes he slips and doesn't make sense.

"Who are you talking about?" I say, and push the sandwich closer. I'm wondering when he's eaten last. I try to calculate that.

"Whitey," my father says. "He touched me." My father's voice is loud, like I've asked him what time it is, who the president is, like he thinks I'm one of his doctors checking to see if he's with it or not.

He's with it.

He knows what he's saying.

Whitey is my father's brother-in-law. Whitey lives in California with my father's second-favorite sister. Whitey and my aunt have always seemed happily married. They live by the ocean. They have a beach house. They still have their pictures taken in California sunsets every year, like high school sweethearts, even though they're both pushing 80. They send the pictures tucked into Christmas cards—"Greetings from paradise! Wish you were here!"

My father calls his sister every Christmas. He calls her on every holiday. He knows the time difference and always calls at 8 p.m. her time—after dinner, after the news, before a good movie might be coming on. This time, 8 p.m., my father figures, is a good time, a considerate time, for his sister to have a chat. It's 11 p.m. our time, my father's time, right when he usually settles in and falls asleep to the TV news.

⇜❦⇝

Because they grew up with two languages, my father and his sister speak to each other in English and Polish. My father never taught me much Polish, so I can't always understand what they're saying.

"We speak American in my house," he likes to say.

"*Kocham cie*," my father always says to his sister, which I know means I love you because it's one of the things my father did teach me. "Repeat it," he'd say as we'd drive to my grandfather's house, and I would. "Again," my father would say, until I'd get it right. I'd walk into my grandfather's house. I'd go up to him. I would not hug him. My grandfather didn't like children, didn't like to be touched. "*Kocham cie,*" I'd say. I'd call him *Gia Gia,* grandfather. I don't remember him ever saying much to me. My grandfather came from Poland. I'm not sure how much English he spoke, what he understood. I know he didn't think of me as one of his real grandchildren. I know he blamed my mother, the gypsy, for not being able to give my father a proper child of his own. I know because sometimes this came up when my parents used to fight. When my parents used to fight, which they don't much anymore, they fought in English. There was no mistaking anything.

"I love you," my father always tells his sister, in the language they shared as kids, and she says it back, I think.

Then she puts her husband on the phone.

⌁⊰⊱⌁

"How you doing, Whitey," my father says, and his voice lowers the way it always does when my father talks to other men. All the men in my family do this, change octaves in each other's presence, the verbal equivalent of a firm handshake.

Whitey is in a wheelchair. He's had many strokes. His name fits. His skin is the color of skim milk. His hair is white blonde, not gray. His eyes are a transparent blue, like something mixed in a test tube. Every few years, Whitey and my aunt make the trip from California back to Pittsburgh. It must be a hard trip, but Whitey in his wheelchair smiles and nods and is agreeable to everything. "He is so pleasant," my aunt says, and she pats his head. "My sweet Whitey. He never complains."

Whitey sits like an oyster and lets my aunt call him pleasant. He has these thick eyebrows that almost meet at the bridge of his nose. The eyebrows make him look long-suffering, which of course he is. This should make him likeable, but he's not and never has been, though I can't say why. As a kid, I never wanted to be alone with him. It wasn't the wheelchair. It was that he seemed like the kind of character from a horror movie who only pretended to need a wheelchair. He seemed like the kind of person who, when other people weren't looking, could get up and walk out to the garage and come back with an ax.

∽⊰∣⊱∾

"Whitey," my father says again. There is the mound of fries between us, untouched. There is the orange plastic tray. The Muzak has shifted to something else, some song I can't name.

I say, "What about Whitey?"

My father pushes his sandwich back at me. "He touched my peepee."

This is the word he uses, and when he says it, my father, so old and close to death, somehow looks like a child.

I say, "What did you say, Dad?"

He repeats it. This time he lowers his voice, deepens it. He looks straight at me, through me, delivering that handshake, handshake. Be a man, the voice says. Say it.

259

"I just thought you should know," he says. "I thought you should know what he did, that son of a bitch. He touched me. He touched my peepee. I was just a kid for Christ's sake."

My father looks at his sandwich. He presses his hand down on the bun and flattens it. He keeps doing that, pressing it down. He says, "Why would he do that?"

All around us, nothing's stopped. The woman with her samples keeps pushing toothpicks at a woman loaded down with Victoria's Secret bags. The Victoria's Secret woman has a son with her. She keeps him on a leash. The leash is stretchy, like a telephone cord, and strapped on the woman's wrist. The boy keeps jerking this way and that, trying to escape. The leash works like a slinky, pulling him back to his mother and her bright pink lingerie, her mouthful of Szechuan chicken. "Knockitoff, Joey," she says between bites, but Joey won't hold still. Nothing in the food court will hold still and I think it should stop, all of it. Everything should freeze and go silent.

My father's sandwich is pressed nearly flat. My father does not look relieved to have told me this. He looks as sad and angry as ever.

"How could anybody do that?" my father asks and he wants an answer.

I don't have an answer and so I say, "I don't know."

I say, "I'm sorry." I say, "Jesus Christ, Dad."

I say, "Why didn't you tell me before?"

And my father says, "I thought you wouldn't believe me."

Back home, I tell my mother what my father said and she nods like I'm reporting the weather.

"I tried to get him help for years but he wouldn't go," she says. "Well, he went one time, but once we got there, he convinced the doctor I was the crazy one."

We're doing dishes. She washes. I dry. My father's back in the bedroom asleep. The trip to the mall has worn him out. All the talking has worn him out. He fell asleep in the car on the drive back. I was relieved I didn't have to say anything because I couldn't think of anything to say.

My mother tells me the full story, all the parts my father left out.

She says, "I think that's why he's always been so miserable."

She says, "He's never been able to get around that."

She says, "We thought maybe adopting you would help."

She says, "He only ever wanted a little girl."

She says, "I think it helped, having you."

She says, "He was never really o.k. though."

46

My father is young, nine, maybe ten. Already he wants to be a singer.

He has a beautiful voice. He was born with a beautiful voice. Everyone says so. The priest, his teachers, his mother who he loves very much, the mother who will die right after my father gets married and his family will blame it on the gypsy curse.

My father's mother calls him *ptaczek*, her little bird. Oh the way he sings. He is his mother's favorite. Being the favorite of ten is no small thing.

He gets his beautiful voice from his mother, though she sings only in church, only for God, and my father wants to be famous, a famous singer. His mother worries about this, his pride, his ambition. She worries it will lead to something terrible for her son. She tells the priest this. The priest says her son's voice is God's gift. She should let him use it.

My father, born poor, wants to be rich. He wants to buy his mother a beautiful house and lace dresses, the kind he's seen her look at in catalogues. He wants money, so much money he'll never have to worry about shoes ever again. Do not get your shoes wet, his father warns. Do not scuff your shoes. Do you think shoes grow on trees? His father beats children over shoes.

My father has seen shoes strung up by their laces high in tree branches and has thought about shoes growing on trees. He's worried about what's happened to the children whose shoes those were, how badly the children suffered over those lost shoes.

He wants to be a famous singer with closets full of shoes.

He has a beautiful voice, a gift from God.

Later he'll win a contest and get to sing on the radio in Braddock, but for now he's just a kid with a dream. Sometimes at school he goes into the bathroom stall and sings a bar or two. *Oh Susannah oh don't you cry for me.* He lets his big voice bounce off the plumbing. He likes the sound of his voice coming back at him, like a reflection.

His oldest sister loves music, too. She doesn't really sing, but she likes musicians. She's always hanging around the clubs. Their father beats her for this, worse than he beats for shoes, but she still sneaks out, goes back, and now she has a new love, a drummer.

My father doesn't know what she sees in this one. The drummer's skin is white and taut, a surgical glove pulled over his cheeks and forehead. He's thin and pasty and his eyes are pale but blue, like cough drops that have been sucked down so they're thin and almost see-through. Everything about him looks like medicine. He has long fingers that wrap around the drum sticks like gauze. They're that white, his fingers, and that's his nickname, too, Whitey. It fits.

264

"Hey sport," Whitey says. He calls everyone sport, my father most of all. "I hear you sing some. How about you give us a few bars, sport? Show us what you got."

My father's sister holds onto the new boyfriend's arm.

She says, "Isn't he just the most pleasant thing?"

Whitey smiles and my father thinks medicine, something mothballed and awful.

Still my father sings a few bars. He can't help but sing when someone wants to hear it.

Whitey says, "That's not bad, sport."

Whitey says, "I think you could sit in with the band sometime. You have real talent."

Whitey says, "I know talent," and gives the sister a squeeze.

"Isn't he the most pleasant man?" she says.

Whitey has his own apartment, with a little music room in the back.

Later, he'll say, "Why don't you get comfortable with that microphone sport?"

He'll say, "Breathe, get comfortable."

He'll say, "You can't sing with your belt buckled tight like that."

He'll say, "Loosen up, Sport. Unbutton a bit."

He'll say, "Relax. No one's going to bite you."

He'll say, "Nothing you can't wash off, right?"

He'll send the sister out for cigarettes. He'll send her out for beer. He'll send her out for a newspaper and a magazine and some new sheet music. She'll come back and giggle and kiss my father on the head. She'll kiss Whitey on the mouth.

She'll say, "Isn't he so pleasant?"

She'll say, "Doesn't my brother have the most beautiful voice? He's an angel."

She won't notice my father's belt on the floor. She won't notice that he's been crying. She won't notice weeks later when he's stopped crying. She won't notice years later that he's stopped singing, or years after that when he calls long-distance to wish her a Merry Christmas, a Happy Birthday, a good New Year and never once asks her to put Whitey on the phone, though she always does. "I'll put Whitey on," she says, as if it's something my father chooses, as if it's something he wants, as if it's something that would make him happy.

47

Because the world failed my father, I thought maybe he wouldn't fight so hard to stay in it. This isn't true. My father will live for weeks after doctors say it is impossible, that his body is shutting down.

"I'm going to live to 100," my father used to say, "I'll live to see the bastards burn."

He didn't sound his usual angry self when he'd say this. He'd say it like he was reciting a math equation, the law of total probability.

The world failed my father.

He wanted to live 100 years, long enough to right that.

⋯⟐⋯

Before he dies, my father slips in and out of a coma. I try not to make too much of a fuss when he is conscious, but once, when I am sure he is out of it, I can't help it. I sit next to him in the spare room where the delivery guy set up the rented hospital bed and weep. I must be making a terrible fuss because my father wakes and turns to me and

267

says, "Don't worry, sweetheart, I'm not going anywhere. I'll be around."

Because I am my father's only child, because he is my father, I believe him.

⊸⟨⟩⟞

"Family," my father said, "is the only thing that matters."

"Without family," my father said, "you've got nothing."

"You have one mother and one father," my father said. "Remember that."

"I'll be around," my father said, and sometimes I think he is.

This makes me feel better, knowing he is somehow still here.

48

ॐ

This year my birthday passes without time to celebrate. No cake, no party. I've been working a lot. Phelan, who is 9 now, refuses to believe I'm a year older because I didn't blow out any candles.

"If you don't blow out your candles, you'll never be 49," she says, a good thought.

These days I wonder a lot about time, how much I've wasted by focusing on the wrong things or the wrong people or the wrong landscapes.

"It's over before you know it," my father used to say about living.

"Patience, jackass." My father used to say that, too.

⊰⊹⊱

Every year for my birthday, my mother would make my favorite cake—red devil's food with maple frosting. It's a difficult recipe, at least that's what she always said.

"Can't you pick something else?" she'd say, and sigh.

"For Christ's sake, do not stomp in the kitchen," she'd say when the cake was in the oven. "This one's sensitive."

"We'll see if it comes out this year," she'd say every year, though every year it would come out just fine.

I'm not sure what the fuss was about, except the recipe was a family one. It came from my grandmother, my mother's mother, who was notorious for leaving out ingredients so no one could duplicate her recipes, which meant no one could ever replace her.

"It's about immortality," I said the other night to my friend, Ed, the poet. We weren't talking about recipes. We were talking about writers, why some people wrote so many books.

"People shouldn't write so much," he said, but I disagree. I think writers should write as much as they can. Not because, as Ed would say, they'd be trying "to write for the ages," but because writing is work and it's what we're made to do. It says, "I was here." It says, "Maybe this life matters a little."

It gives us purpose and makes us useful.

꼯

Here's my grandmother's recipe for that cake, exactly as my mother typed it out on the typewriter she and my father gave me when I was in 8th grade. I still have the typewriter. It was the greatest gift I ever received because it meant my parents believed in me and what I loved.

RED DEVILS FOOD CAKE 1 ½ Receipt

2-1/4 c. sugar (cream good)

3/c c. spry (add eggs)
3 eggs
3 scant tbls. Cocoa + a little more
3 c. flour—sift 3 times
1-1/2 c. buttermilk
1-1/2 teas. Soda
1-1/2 teas. Vanilla
1-1/2 tbl. White vinegar
Pinch salt
1-1/2 ounce red coloring
Pour in well greased pans. Bake at 350 for 30 to 35 min.

My mother typed *recipe* as *receipt*, which is right, I think—recipe as proof of an exchange, a transaction between generations. But it's the vagueness—cream good, plus a little more, sift 3 times—that bugs me. It sounds like magic, like something I'd learned in New Orleans when I visited the Voodoo Museum and put a wish in a tree stump. I wrote the wish on an index card, a recipe card. I used a tiny pencil stub.

I made two wishes, actually. They read:

1)   I wish my father a good death.

2)   I wish to be happy.

I put these wishes, with all their seriousness, into a fake plastic tree stump in a shop full of voodoo-doll key chains, sandwich-bagged potions, and dead snakes floating in jars of formaldehyde. It was all a joke, but it wasn't.

I was sad. My father was dying.

I wished him a good death although I knew there

was no such thing. I wished for happiness, but I'd hung a quote by Colette above my writing workspace. "Who said you should be happy? Do your work."

This was a few months before I turned 35. I was floating in my own little jar.

≈≈

I was home that year for my birthday. My father would die two weeks later, my mother five years after that. My father hadn't been eating much. Still, we were a family that believed in things, so my mother made the red devil's food cake.

"For Christ's sake, don't stomp," she said, but she sounded exhausted. She'd been taking care of my father for a long time. I'd moved home to help with the end. People called me a good daughter.

As for the cake, it came out perfect and delicious. My mother lined it with candles.

"We'll count in fives," she said, and put seven candles on top. "We don't want to burn the house down."

My father got up from his rented hospital bed. He walked to the kitchen. He sat in his chair at the far end of the table. He asked for a piece of cake. A big piece.

"Delicious," he said, though he ate only a few bites.

This is one of my last memories of the three of us together as a family. This is my last memory of my father, fully conscious, his knit cap pulled low over his forehead, even so close to death embarrassed by what cancer had done to his hair.

"Here's to happiness, sweetheart," he said and raised his fork in a toast.

49

My father is underground in Braddock, not far from the steel mill. I talk to him the way people talk to their dead. When I have a good day, I tell him something beautiful about the grandchildren he never knew. When I have a bad day, I tell him the world is a shitty place, that it's not just me. I tell him a paranoid's favorite joke: "Humpty Dumpty was pushed." I tell him everyone I know has fallen—no, was pushed—and the world is worse than ever and he was right about a lot of things.

⊷⊰}⊱⊶

No matter how my father's day went, no matter how tired he was, every evening he would sit at the kitchen table and tear stale bread to feed the birds. Sometimes still in his work clothes, still filthy with graphite, he put bread in a feeder he built from scrap wood and hung in the maple tree in our yard. He threw the rest of the bread in the air and shook the crumbs from the bag and then stood back and waited for the birds, ordinary sparrows mostly, to come down like a curtain around him.

"They wait for me," he'd say, "they know I'm coming," and I think he was right because the birds chirped and sang and filled the shrubs around our house every day at the same time. When the birds saw my father come out of the garage with his plastic bag full, the shrubs shook and the birdsong would get so loud it drowned out the cars on Route 130.

I tell my dead father I remember that, too.

❧

Today I tell my father about the painted-lady butterflies Phelan's keeping in her room. She mail-ordered caterpillars—part of a science project she's doing for school—and together we've watched them transform. There were six caterpillars. Five butterflies have hatched so far. The sixth chrysalis fell, so we followed the directions and nestled it on a napkin against the side of the butterfly cage. One of the other butterflies has been staying next to it since yesterday, keeping watch, maybe, worrying, who knows.

I like to think the chrysalis will open, despite the odds. I like to think later today my daughter will come home and find six butterflies.

❧

Phelan takes singing lessons. She loves to sing, and wants to be a famous singer. The voice teacher is puzzled by my daughter's perfect pitch. He watches her sing, smiles, and shakes his head in disbelief.

He says, "Where does she get that from?"

When I tell my daughter she's like her grandfather, she says, "I wish I could have met him." When she asks if her grandfather would have liked her, I say yes, very much.

⚜

Last night before she went to sleep, Phelan said, "I think he's going to make it," meaning the butterfly, and I said, "I hope so."

EPILOGUE

 ॐ

I've tried to make a book of my life, just like my favorite writers have done, just like my least favorite writers have done. I've written and rewritten and revised the first pages because they were blank. All first pages are blank, of course, but for adopted people more so.

Most people ask their parents and their parents sketch in the details. Their parents tell stories and those stories are called true and those stories shape a life and that life is handed down in more stories and so on.

To sketch in the details of what was lost to me, I've asked a social worker, the woman from Catholic Charities. I've asked reports and documents and my imagination. I've asked my dead parents. I've asked why. I've asked how. I've asked my brother, my brother by birth, the one who found me.

As for my brother and I, we have settled into normalcy. We'll have beers at Fat Heads or around our kitchen tables. We'll listen to the Pogues and Bob Dylan. We'll high-five each other when we say or hear something true.

When people ask we say we didn't grow up together, that's all.

I've never met my birth mother. I could, but I don't need or want to anymore. My brother and I don't talk about her much, as if our lives, which started with her, can only go on without her.

Once, earlier, before we understood each other, he held his phone to my ear. It was a voice message, my birth mother calling him to come fix a broken toilet.

"I know you're there, don't ignore me," she said. Her voice was not as rough as I'd imagined. I needed it to be rough.

"Don't do that," I said.

"I thought you'd want to hear her," my brother said. She sounded exactly like a mother, like anyone's mother, calling her grown child. She sounded like what she was to me, a stranger.

Blonde4Eva has a new job, a union job, a good job, and she's happy. She sent an e-mail to tell me. The e-mail was not written in caps or highlighted in green and I wrote back to say I was happy to know this. We still haven't met. I haven't met my other brother, either. I think meeting more people, blood or not, would take away from the time I have with the people I already love.

The sister I met in Fat Head's Saloon is married now, a stepmother. She wants a baby of her own. When she says this, I know what she means and coming from her it sounds right. It sounds fine. I tell her she'll be a good mother because I know how important it is to hear it.

My mother and father are buried together in the Catholic cemetery in Braddock. They share a granite headstone engraved with two small birds and those words

Together Forever. Braddock now is not the Braddock my parents knew. The sign for Guentert's, the fancy bakery where my parents bought their wedding cake, is faded, the shop itself closed for years. Bell's Meat Market, alone in an otherwise vacant lot, runs specials on goat meat. In off hours, there are bars on the windows and doors. UPMC tore down Braddock Hospital where my mother was a nurse. A sign stands where the building used to be, some architect's plans, but for now there's only dirt. The sidewalk in front where my parents set their love story is cracked and broken.

It doesn't matter much. When I visit my parents' graves, I hear gunshots. At night, the fire and lights from the factory, where they still make steel, where work still pays, look like their own city.

People who are born here call it beautiful.

ABOUT THE AUTHOR

Lori Jakiela is the author of the memoirs *Miss New York Has Everything* and *The Bridge to Take When Things Get Serious*, as well as the poetry collection *Spot the Terrorist*. Her work has been published in *The New York Times*, *The Washington Post*, *The Chicago Tribune*, *The Pittsburgh Post-Gazette*, *The Rumpus*, *Brevity* and more. She lives in Pittsburgh with her husband, the writer Dave Newman, and their children. A former flight attendant and journalist, she now teaches in the writing programs at The University of Pittsburgh-Greensburg and Chatham University, and is a co-director of Chautauqua Institution's Summer Literary Festival.

New *and* Forthcoming Releases

Cage of Lit Glass by Charles Kell ❋ Winner of the 2018 Autumn House Poetry Prize, selected by Kimiko Hahn

Not Dead Yet and Other Stories by Hadley Moore ❋ Winner of the 2018 Autumn House Fiction Prize, selected by Dana Johnson

Limited by Body Habitus: An American Fat Story by Jennifer Renee Blevins ❋ Winner of the 2018 Autumn House Nonfiction Prize, selected by Daisy Hernández

Belief Is Its Own Kind of Truth, Maybe by Lori Jakiela

Epithalamia by Erinn Batykefer ❋ Winner of the 2018 Autumn House Chapbook Prize, selected by Gerry LaFemina

Fire and Rain: New and Selected Poems by Patricia Jabbeh Wesley

Heartland Calamitous by Michael Credico

Voice Message by Katherine Barrett Swett ❋ Winner of the 2019 Donald Justice Poetry Prize, selected by Erica Dawson

The Gutter Spread Guide to Prayer by Eric Tran ❋ Winner of the 2019 Rising Writer Prize, selected by Stacey Waite

FOR OUR FULL CATALOG PLEASE VISIT <u>AUTUMNHOUSE.ORG</u>